A DOMINIE IN DOUBT

First published 1921
This edition published by Lector House in 2024

ISBN: 978-93-6138-505-6

Lector House LLP
Registered Office: H. No. 96, Block C, Tomar Colony,
Burari, Delhi – 110084, India
info@lectorhouse.com
www.lectorhouse.com

A DOMINIE IN DOUBT

ALEXANDER SUTHERLAND NEILL

2024

LECTOR HOUSE LLP

A DOMINIE IN DOUBT

BY

A. S. NEILL, M.A.

DEDICATION.

To Homer Lane, whose first lecture convinced me that I knew nothing about education. I owe much to him, but I hasten to warn educationists that they must not hold him responsible for the views given in these pages. I never understood him fully enough to expound his wonderful educational theories.

A. S. N.

Forfar,
August 12, 1920.

CONTENTS

A DOMINIE IN DOUBT

I.

"Just give me your candid opinion of *A Dominie's* Log; I'd like to hear it."

Macdonald looked up from digging into the bowl of his pipe with a dilapidated penknife. He is now head-master of Tarbonny Public School, a school I know well, for I taught in it for two years as an ex-pupil teacher.

Six days ago he wrote asking me to come and spend a holiday with him, so I hastily packed my bag and made for Euston.

This evening had been a sort of complimentary dinner in my honour, the guests being neighbouring dominies and their wives, none of whom I knew. We had talked of the war, of rising prices, and a thousand other things. Suddenly someone mentioned education, and of course my unfortunate *Log* had come under discussion.

I had been anxious to continue my discussion with a Mrs. Brown on the subject of the relative laying values of Minorcas and Buff Orpingtons, but I had been dragged into the miserable business in spite of myself.

Now they were all gone, and Macdonald had returned to the charge.

"It's hardly a fair question," said Mrs. Macdonald, "to ask an author what he thinks of his own book. No man can judge his own work, any more than a mother can judge her own child."

"That's true!" I said. "A man can't judge his own behaviour, and writing a book is an element of behaviour. Besides, there is a better reason why a writer cannot judge his own work," I added.

"Because he never reads it?" queried Macdonald with a grin.

I shook my head.

"An author has no further interest in his book after it is published."

Macdonald looked across at me. It was clear that he doubted my seriousness.

"Surely you don't mean to say that you have no interest in *A Dominie's Log*?"

"None whatever!" I said.

"You mean it?" persisted Macdonald.

"My dear Mac," I said, "an author dare not read his own book."

"Dare not! Why?"

"Because it's out of date five minutes after it's written."

For fully a minute we smoked in silence. Macdonald appeared to be digesting my remark.

"You see," I continued presently, "when I read a book on education, I want to learn, and I certainly don't expect to learn anything from the man I was five years ago."

"I think I understand," said Macdonald. "You have come to realise that what you wrote five years ago was wrong. That it?"

"True for you, Mac. You've just hit it."

"You needn't have waited five years to find that out," he said, with a good-natured grin. "I could have told you the day the book was published—I bought one of the first copies."

"Still," he continued, "I don't see why a book should be out-of-date in five years. That is if it deals with the truth. Truth is eternal."

"What is truth?" I asked wearily. "We all thought we knew the truth about gravitation. Then Einstein came along with his relativity theory, and told us we were wrong."

"Did he?" inquired Macdonald, with a faint smile.

"I am quoting from the newspapers," I added hastily. "I haven't the remotest idea what relativity means. Perhaps it's Epstein I mean—no, he's a sculptor."

"You're hedging!" said Macdonald.

"Can you blame me?" I asked. "You're trying to get me to say what truth is. I am not a professor of philosophy, I'm a dominie. All I can say is that the *Log* was the truth . . . for me . . . five years ago; but it isn't the truth for me now."

"Then, what exactly is your honest opinion of the *Log* as a work on education?"

"As a work on education," I said deliberately, "the *Log* isn't worth a damn."

"Not a bad criticism, either," said Macdonald dryly.

"I say that," I continued, "because when I wrote it I knew nothing about the most important factor in education—the psychology of children."

"But," said Mrs. Macdonald in surprise—hitherto she had been an interested listener—"I thought that the bits about the bairns were the best part of the book."

"Possibly," I answered, "but I was looking at children from a grown-up point of view. I thought of them as they affected me, instead of as they affected themselves. I'll give you an instance. I think I said something about wanting to chuck woodwork and cookery out of the school curriculum. I was wrong, hopelessly wrong."

"I'm glad to hear you admit it," said Macdonald. "I have always thought that every boy ought to be taught to mend a hen-house and every girl to cook a dinner."

"Then I was right after all," I said quickly.

Macdonald stared at me, whilst his wife looked up interrogatively from her embroidery.

"If your aim is to make boys joiners and girls cooks," I explained, "then I still hold that cookery and woodwork ought to be chucked out of the schools."

"But, man, what are schools for?" I saw a combative light in Macdonald's eye.

"Creation, self-expression .... the only thing that matters in education. I don't care what a child is doing in the way of creation, whether he is making tables, or porridge, or sketches, or—or—"

"Snowballs!" prompted Macdonald.

"Or snowballs," I said. "There is more true education in making a snowball than in listening to an hour's lecture on grammar."

Mrs. Macdonald dropped her embroidery into her lap, with a little gasp at the heresy of my remark.

"You're talking pure balderdash!" said Macdonald, leaning forward to knock the ashes from his pipe on the bars of the grate.

"Very well," I said cheerfully. "Let's discuss it. You make a class sit in front of you for an hour, and you threaten to whack the first child that doesn't pay attention to your lesson on nouns and pronouns."

"Discipline," said Macdonald.

"I don't care what you call it. I say it's stupidity."

"But, hang it all, man, you can't teach if you haven't got the children's attention."

"And you can't teach when you have got it," I said. "A child learns only when it is interested."

"But surely, discipline makes them interested," said Mrs. Macdonald.

I shook my head. "It only makes them attentive."

"Same thing," said Macdonald.

"No, Mac," I replied. "It is not the same thing. Attention means the applying of the conscious mind to a thing; interest means the application of both the conscious and the unconscious mind. When you force a child to attend to a lesson for fear of the tawse, you merely engage the least important part of his mind—the conscious. While he stares at the blackboard his unconscious is concerned with other things."

"What sort of things?" asked Macdonald.

"Very probably his unconscious is working out an elaborate plan to murder you," I said, "and I don't blame it either," I added.

"And the snowballs?" queried Mrs. Macdonald.

"When a boy makes a snowball, he is interested; his whole soul is in the job, that is, his unconscious and his conscious are working together. For the moment he is an artist, a creator."

"So that's the new education . . . making snowballs?" said Macdonald.

"It isn't really," I said; "but what I want to do is to point out that making snowballs is nearer to true education than the spoon-feeding we call education to-day."

* * * * *

Duncan does not like me. He is a young dominie of twenty-three or thereabouts, a friend of Macdonald, and he has just been demobilised. He was a major, and he does not seem to have recovered from the experience. He has got what the vulgar call swelled head. Last night he was dilating upon the delinquencies of the old retired teacher who ran the school while Duncan was on active service. It seems that the old man had allowed the school to run to seed.

"Would you believe it," I overheard Duncan say to Macdonald, "when I came back I found that the boys and girls were playing in the same playground. Why, man, some of them were playing on the road! And the discipline! Awful!"

Poor children! I see it all; I see Duncan line them up like a squad of recruits, and march them into school with never a smile on their faces or a word on their lips. Macdonald tells me that he makes them lift their slates by numbers.

And the amusing thing is that Duncan thinks himself one of the more advanced teachers. He reads the educational journals, and eagerly devours the articles about new methods in teaching arithmetic and geography. His school is only a mile and a half away, and I hope that he will come over to see Mac a few times while I am here.

I have seen the old type of dominie, and I have seen the new type. I prefer the former. He had many faults, but he usually managed to do something for the human side of the children. The new type is a danger to children. The old dominie leathered the children so that they might make a good show before the inspector; the new dominie leathers them because he thinks that children ought to be disciplined so that they may be able to fight the battle of life. He does not see that by using authority he is doing the very opposite of what he intends; he is making the child dependent on him, and for ever afterwards the child will lack initiative, lack self-confidence, lack originality.

What the new dominie does do is to turn out excellent wage-slaves. The discipline of the school gives each child an inner sense of inferiority . . . . what the psycho-analysts call an inferiority complex. And the working-classes are suffering from a gigantic inferiority complex . . . . otherwise they would not be content to remain wage-slaves. The fear that Duncan inspires in a boy will remain in that boy all his life. When he enters the workshop he will unconsciously identify the foreman with Duncan, and fear him and hate him. I believe that many a strike is really a vague insurrection against the teacher. For it is well known that the unconscious mind is infantile.

* * * * *

To-night I dropped in to see my old friend Dauvit Todd the cobbler. Many an evening have I spent in his dirty shop. Dauvit works on after teatime, and the village worthies gather round his fire and smoke and spit and grunt. I have sat there for an hour many a night, and not a single word was said. Peter Smith the blacksmith would give a great sigh and say: "Imphm!" There would be silence for ten minutes, and then Jake Tosh the roadman would stare at the fire, shake his head, and say: "Aye, man!" Then a ploughman would smack his lips and say: "Man, aye!" A southerner looking in might have jumped to the conclusion that the assembly was collectively and individually bored, but boredom never enters Dauvit's shop. We Scots think better in crowds.

To-night the old gang was there. The hypothetical southerner again would have marvelled at the reception I received. I walked into the shop after an absence of five years.

"Weel, Dauvit," I said, and sat down in the basket chair. Dauvit and I have never shaken hands in our lives. He looked up.

"Back again!" he said, without any evident surprise; then he added: "And what like a nicht is 't ootside?"

Gradually other men dropped in, and the same sort of greeting took place. The weather continued to be discussed for a time. Then the blacksmith said: "Auld Tam Davidson's swine dee'd last nicht."

Dauvit looked up from the boot he was repairing.

"What did it dee o'?" and there followed an argument about the symptoms of swine fever.

An English reader of *The House with the Green Shutters* would have concluded that these villagers were deliberately trying to put me in my place. By ignoring me might they not be showing their contempt for dominies who have just come from London? Not they. They were glad to see me again, and their method of showing their gladness was to take up our friendship at the point where it left off five years ago.

The only time a Scot distrusts other Scots is when they fuss over him. The story goes in Tarbonny that when young Jim Lunan came home unexpectedly after a ten years' farming in Canada, his mother was washing the kitchen floor.

"Mother!" he cried, "I've come hame!"

She looked over her shoulder.

"Wipe yer feet afore ye come in, ye clorty laddie," she said.

But there is a garrulous type of Scot . . . or rather the type of Scot that tries to make the other fellow garrulous. In our county we call them the speerin' bodie. To speer means to ask questions. The speerin' bodie is common enough in Fife, and I suppose it was a Fifer who entered a railway compartment one morning and sat down to study the only other occupant—an Englishman.

"It's a fine day," said the Scot, and there was a question in his tone.

The Englishman sighed and laid aside his newspaper.

"Aye, mester," continued the inquisitive Fifer, "and ye'll be——"

The Englishman held up a forbidding hand.

"You needn't go on," he said; "I'll tell you everything about myself. I was born in Leeds, the son of poor parents. I left school at the age of twelve, and I became a draper. I gradually worked my way up, and now I am traveller for a Manchester firm. I married six years ago. Three kids. Wife has rheumatism. Willie had measles last month. I have a seven room cottage; rent £27. I vote Tory; go to the Baptist church, and keep hens. Anything else you want to know?"

The Scot had a very dissatisfied look.

"What did yer grandfaither dee o'?" he demanded gruffly.

When the argument about swine fever had died down, Dauvit turned to me.

"Aye, and how is Lunnon lookin'?"

"Same as ever," I answered.

"Ye'll have to tak' Dauvit doon on a trip," laughed the smith.

Dauvit drove in a tacket.

"Man, smith, I was in Lunnon afore you was born," he said.

"Go on, Dauvit," I said encouragingly, "tell us the story." I had heard it before, but I longed to hear it again. Dauvit brightened up.

"There's no muckle to tell," he said, as he tossed the boot into a corner and wiped his face with his apron. "It'll be ten years come Martimas. Me and Will Tamson gaed up by boat frae Dundee. Oh! we had a graund time. But there's no muckle to tell."

"What about Dave Brownlee?" I asked.

Dauvit chuckled softly.

"But ye've a' heard the story," he said, but we protested that we hadn't.

"Aweel," he began, "some of you will no doubt mind o' Dave Broonlee him that stoppit at Millend. Dave served his time as a draper, and syne he got a good job in a Lunnon shop. Weel, me and Will Tamson was walkin' along the Strand when Will he says to me, says he: 'Cud we no pay a veesit to Dave Broonlee?' Then I minded that Dave's father had said something aboot payin' him a call, but I didna ken his address. All I kent was that he was in a big shop in Oxford Street.

"Weel, Will and me we goes up to a bobby and speers the way to Oxford Street. When we got there Will he goes up to another bobby and says: 'Please cud ye tell me whatna shop Dave Broonlee works intil?' At that I started to laugh, and syne the bobby he started to laugh. He laughed a lang time and syne when I telt him that it was a draper's shop he directed us to a great big muckle shop wi' a thousand windows.

"'Try there first,' says the bobby.

"Weel, in we goes, and a mannie in a tail coat he comes forart rubbin' his hands.

"'And what can I do for you, sir?' he says to Will.

"'Oh,' says Will, 'we want to see Dave Broonlee,' but the man didna ken what Will was sayin'. It took Will and me twenty meenutes to get him to onderstand.

"'Oh,' says he, 'I understand now. You want to see Mr. Brownlee?'

"'Ye're fell quick in the uptak,' says Will, but of coorse the man didna ken what he was sayin'.

"He went to the backshop to speer aboot Dave, and when he cam back he says, says he: 'I'm sorry, but Mr. Brownlee has gone out to lunch. Will you leave a message?'

"Will turned to the door.

"'Never mind,' says he, 'we'll see him doon the toon.'"

* * * * *

In reading my *Log* I am appalled by the amount of lecturing I did in school. Since writing it I have visited most of the best schools in England, and I found that I was not the only teacher who lectured. But we are all wrong. I fancy that the real reason why I lectured so much was to indulge my showing-off propensities. To stand before a class or an audience; to be the cynosure of all eyes; to have a crowd hanging on your words .... all showing off! Very, very human, but .... bad for the audience.

When a teacher lectures he is unconsciously giving expression to his desire to gain a feeling of superiority. That, I fancy, is the deepest wish of every one of us .... to impress others, to be superior. You see it in the smallest child. Give him an audience, and he will show off for hours. The boy at the top of the class gains his feeling of superiority by beating the others at arithmetic, while the dunce at the bottom of the class gains his in more original ways ... punching the top boy at playtime, scoring goals at football, spitting farther than anyone else in school. I have seen a boy smash a window merely to draw attention to himself, and thus to gain a momentary feeling of superiority.

And we grown-ups are boys at heart. The boy is the father to the man. Take, for instance, a childish trait—exhibitionism. Most children at an early age love to run about naked, to show off their bodies. Later the conventions of society make the child repress this wish to exhibit himself. But we know that a repressed wish does not die; it merely buries itself in the unconscious. Many years later the exhibition impulse comes out in sublimated form as a desire to show off before the public ... hence our politicians, actors, actresses, street-corner revivalists, and—er—dominies.

Now I hasten to add that there is nothing to be ashamed of in being a politician or a dominie. But if I lecture a class I am making the affair my show, and I am not the most important actor in the play; I am the scene-shifter; the real actors who should be declaiming their lines are sitting on hard benches staring at me and wondering what I am raving about. Each little person is thirsting to show his or her superiority, and he never gets the chance. Occasionally I may ask a sleepy-looking urchin what are the exports to Canada, and he may gain a slight feeling of superiority if he can tell the right answer. Yet I fancy that his unconscious self despises me and my question. Why in all the earth should I ask a question when I know the answer? The whole thing is an absurdity. The only questions asked in a school should be asked by the pupils.

The truth is that our schools do not give education; they give instruction. And it is so very easy to instruct, and so very easy to go on talking, and so very easy to whack Tommy when he does not listen. Our prosy lectures are wasted time. The children would be better employed playing marbles.

Of course if a child asks for information that is a different story. He is obviously interested . . . that is if he isn't trying to tempt you into a long explanation so that you will forget to hear his Latin verbs. Children soon understand our little vanities, and they soon learn to exploit them.

* * * * *

"I had a scene in school to-day," remarked Mac while we were at tea to-night.

"What happened?" I asked.

"Tom Murray was wrong in all his sums, and he wouldn't hold out his hand," and by Mac's grim smile I knew that the bold Tom had been conquered.

"What would you have done in a case like that?" asked Mac.

"I would never have a case like that, Mac. If he had all his sums wrong I should sit down and ask myself what was wrong with my teaching."

"I didn't mean that," he said; "what I meant was: what would you do if Tom defied you?"

"That wouldn't happen either, Mac. Tom couldn't defy me because you can only defy an authority, and I'm not an authority."

Mac shook his head.

"You won't convince me, old chap. A boy like Tom has to be dealt with with a firm hand."

I studied his face for a time.

"You know, Mac," I said, "you puzzle me. You're one of the kindest decentest chaps in the world, and yet you go leathering poor Tom Murray. Why do you do it?"

"You must keep discipline," he said.

I shook my head.

"Mac, if you knew yourself you wouldn't ever whack a child."

This seemed to tickle him.

"Good Lord!" he laughed, "I could write a book about myself! I'm one of the most introspective chaps ever born."

"And you understand yourself?"

"I have no illusions about myself at all, old chap. I know my limitations."

"Well, would you mind telling me why you are a bit of a nut?" I asked. "It isn't usual for a country dominie to wear a wing collar, a bow tie, and shot-silk socks."

"That's easy," he said quickly. "I think that teachers haven't the social standing they ought to have, and I dress well to uphold the dignity of the profession. Don't you believe me?" he demanded as I smiled.

"Quite! I believe you're quite honest in your belief, but it's wrong you know. There must be a much more personal reason than that."

"Rot!" he said. "Anyway, what is the reason?"

"I don't know, Mac; it would take months of research to discover it. I can't explain your psychology, but I'll tell you something about my own. These swagger corduroys I'm wearing . . . when I bought them someone asked me why I chose corduroy, and I at once answered: 'Economy! They'll last ten years!' But that wasn't the real reason, I bought them because I wanted to have folk stare at me. I've got an inferiority complex, that is an inner feeling of inferiority. To compensate for it I go and order a suit that will make people look at me; in short, that I may be the centre of all eyes, and thus gain a feeling of outward superiority."

This sent Mac off into a roar of laughter.

"You're daft, man!" he roared.

After a minute or two he said; "But what has all this to do with Tom Murray?"

"A lot," I said seriously. "You think you whack Tom because you must have discipline, but you whack him for a different reason. In your deep unconscious mind you are an infant. You want to show your self-assertion just as a kid does. You leather Tom because you've never outgrown your seven-year-old stage. On market-day, when Tom walks behind a drove and whacks the stots over the hips with a stick, he is doing exactly what you did this afternoon. You are both infants."

I have had to give up lecturing Mac, for he always takes me as a huge joke. He is a good fellow, but he has the wonderful gift of being blind to anything that might make him reconsider his values. Many people protect themselves in the same way—by laughing. I have more than once seen an alcoholic laugh heartily at his wrecked home and lost job.

II.

What an amount of excellent material Mac and his kind are spoiling. Tom Murray is a fine lad, full of energy and initiative, but he has to sit passive at a desk doing work that does not interest him. His creative faculties have no outlet at all during the day, and naturally when free from authority at nights he expresses his creative interest anti-socially. He nearly wrecked the five-twenty the other night; he tied a huge iron bolt to the rails. Mac called it devilment, but it was merely curiosity. He had had innumerable pins and farthings flattened on the line, and he wanted to see what the engine really could do.

There is devilment in some of Tom's activities, for example in his deliberate destruction of Dauvit's apple tree. Mac and the law would give him the birch for that, but fortunately Mac and the law don't know who did it. Tom's destructiveness is only the direct result of Mac's authority. Suppression always has the same result; it turns a young god into a young devil. Had I Tom in a free school all his activities would be social and good.

And yet nearly every teacher believes in Mac's way. They suppress all the time, and what is worst of all they firmly believe they are doing the best thing.

"Look at Glasgow!" cried Mac the other night when I was talking about the crime of authority. "Look at Glasgow! What happened there during the war? Juvenile crime increased. And why? Because the fathers were in the army and the boys had no control over them; they broke loose. That proves that your theories are potty."

I believe that juvenile crime did increase during the war, and I believe that Mac's explanation of the phenomenon is correct. The absence of the father gave the boy liberty to be a hooligan. But no boy wants to be a hooligan unless he has a strong rebellion against authority. No boy is destructive if he is free to be constructive. I think that the difference between Mac and myself is this: he believes in original sin, while I believe in original virtue.

I wonder why it is so difficult to convert the authority people to the new way of thinking. There must be a deep reason why they want to cling to their authority. Authority gives much power, and love of power may be at the root of the desire to retain authority. Yet I fancy that it is deeper than that. In Mac, for instance, I think that his quickness in becoming angry at Tom's insubordination is due to the insubordination within himself. Like most of us Mac has a father complex, and he fears and hates any authority exercised over himself. So in squashing Tom's rebellion he is unconsciously squashing the rebellion in his own soul. Tom's rebellion could not affect me because I have got rid of my father complex, and his rebellion would touch nothing in me.

Authority will be long in dying, for too many people cling to it as a prop. Most people like to have their minds made up for them; it is so easy to obey orders, and so difficult to live your own life carrying your own burden and finding your own path. To live your own life . . . that is the ideal. To discover yourself bravely, to realise yourself fully, to follow truth even if the crowd stone you. That is living . . . but it is dangerous living, for that way lies crucifixion. No one in authority has ever been crucified; every martyr dies because he challenges authority. . . Christ, Thomas More, Jim Connolly.

* * * * *

Duncan and McTaggart the minister were in to-night, and we got on to the subject of wit and humour. Having a psycho-analysis complex I mentioned the theory that we laugh so as to give release to our repressions. The others shook their heads, and I decided to test my theory on them. I told them the story of the golfer who was driving off about a foot in front of the teeing marks. The club secretary happened to come along.

"Here, my man!" cried the indignant secretary, "you're disqualified!"

"What for?" demanded the player.

"You're driving off in front of the teeing mark."

The player looked at him pityingly.

"Away, you bletherin' idiot!" he said tensely, "I'm playing my third!"

"Now," I said to the others, "I'm going to tell you one by one what your golf is like. You, McTaggart, are a scratch man or a plus man. Is that so?"

"Plus one," he said in surprise. "How did you guess?"

"I didn't guess," I said with great superiority. "I found out by pure science. You didn't laugh at my joke; you merely smiled. That shows that bad golf doesn't touch any complex inside you. The man who takes three strokes to make one foot of ground means nothing to you because, as I say, there's nothing in yourself it touches."

"Wonderful!" cried the minister.

"It's quite simple," I crowed, "and now for Mac! You, Mac, are a rotten player; you take sixteen to a hole."

"Only ten," protested Mac hastily. "How the devil did you know? I've never played with you."

"Deduction, my boy. You roared at my joke, because it touched your bad golf complex. In fact you were really laughing at yourself and your own awful golf."

"What about me?" put in Duncan.

Now there was something in Duncan's eye that should have warned me of danger, but I was so proud of my success that I plunged confidently.

"Oh, you don't play golf," I said airily.

"Wrong!" he cried, "I do! And I'm worse than Mac too!"

I was astounded.

"Impossible!" I cried. "You never laughed at my story at all; that is it touched nothing whatsoever inside you."

Duncan shook his head.

"You're completely wrong this time."

"Well, why *didn't* you laugh?" I asked.

He grinned.

"I dunno. Possibly it is because I first heard that joke in my cradle."

* * * * *

Mac's infant mistress was off duty to-day owing to an attack of influenza, and he gladly accepted my offer to take her place.

Half-an-hour after my entry into the room Mac came in to see how I was getting on. Most of the infants were swarming over me, and Mac frowned. At his frown they all crept back silently to their seats.

"You seem to have the fatal gift of demoralising children," he growled.

It hadn't struck me before, but it is a fact; I do demoralise children. Not long ago I entered a Montessori school, and I spoke not one word. In five minutes the insets and long stairs were lying neglected in the middle of the floor, and the kiddies were scrambling over me. I felt very guilty for I feared that if Montessori herself were to walk in she would be indignant. I cannot explain why I affect kiddies in this way. It may be that intuitively they know that I do not inspire fear or respect; it may be that they unconsciously recognise the baby in me. Anyway, as Mac says, it is a fatal gift.

I think Miss Martin the infant mistress is a good teacher. Her infants do not fear her, and I am sure they love her. The only person they fear is Mac, poor dear old Mac, the most lovable soul in the world. He tries hard to show his love for the infants but somehow they know that behind his smile is the grim head-master who leathers Tom Murray. I sent wee Mary Smith into Mac's room to fetch some chalk to-day, and she wept and feared to enter. Occasionally, I believe, Mac will enter the room, seize a wee mite who is speaking instead of working, and give him or her a scud with the tawse. I wonder how a good soul like Mac can do it.

I have an unlovely story of a board school. An infant mistress lay dying, and in her delirium she cried in terror lest her head-master should come in again and strap her dear, wee infants. It is a true story, and it is the most damning indictment of board school education anyone could wish for. She was a good woman who loved children, and if fear of her head-master brought terror to her on her deathbed, what terrors are such men inspiring in poor wee infants? The men who beat children are exactly in the position of the men who stoned Jesus Christ; they know not what they do, nor do they know why they do it.

* * * * *

There was a stranger in Dauvit's shop when I entered to-day, a seedy-looking whiskered man with a threadbare coat and extremely dirty linen. Shabby genteel would be the Scots description of him.

Dauvit asked me a casual question about London, and the stranger became interested at once.

"Ah," he said, "you're from London, are ye? Man, yon's a great place, a wonderful place!"

I nodded assent.

"Man," he continued, "yon's the place for sichts! Could anything beat the procession at the Lord Mayor's show, eh?"

I meekly admitted that I had never seen the Lord Mayor's show, and he raised his eyebrows in surprise.

"But I'll tell ye what's just as good, mister, and that's the King and Queen opening Parliament. Man, yon's a sicht, isn't it?"

"I—er—I haven't had the opportunity of seeing it," I said.

He looked more surprised than ever.

"But, man, I'll tell ye what's just as good, and that's a big London fire. Man, to see the way the firemen go up the ladders like monkeys. Yon's a sicht for sair een!"

"I never had the luck to see a fire in London," I said hesitatingly. "When were you last in town?"

He did not seem to hear my question; he was evidently thinking of other London thrills.

"Man," he said ruminatingly, "often while I sit in the Tarbonny Kirk I just sit and think aboot Westminster Abbey. Man, yon's a kirk! I suppose you'll be there ilka Sunday?"

I found it difficult to tell him that I had never been in the Abbey, but I managed to get the words out, and then I avoided his reproachful eye. He knocked out his pipe, and I took the action to be a symbolic one meaning: You are an empty sort of person. He studied me critically for a time, then he brightened.

"Aye," he said cheerfully, "London's a graund place, but, for sichts give me New York."

I felt more humble than ever, for I had never travelled. He seemed to guess that by the look of me, for he never asked my opinion of New York.

"Man," he said warmly, "yon's a place! Yon skyscrapers! Phew!" and he whistled his wonder and admiration. "And the streets! Man, ye canna walk on the sidewalk at the busy times. A wonderfu' place, New York, but, as for me, give me the West, California and 'Frisco."

"You have travelled much, sir," I said reverently. The "sir" seemed to come naturally; my inferiority complex was touched on the raw.

Again he ignored me.

"To see yon cowboys! Man, yon's what I call riding! And the Indians!"

He sighed; it was obvious that he was living over again his life in the western wilds. A wistful look crept into his eyes, and I began to construct his sad story. He loved a maid, but the bruiser of the camp loved her also . . . hence the broken-down clothes, the dirty collar. But anon he cheered up again.

"Yes," he said, "I love the West, but for colour and climate give me Japan."

I was so confused now that I had to blow out my pipe vigorously. I glanced at Dauvit, but he was sharpening his knife on the emery hone, and did not appear to be interested. I felt a vague anger against Dauvit; why wasn't he helping me in my trial?

"Japan," continued the irrepressible stranger, "is one of the finest countries in the world, but, for climate give me Siberia."

I hastily thought to myself that if I were Lenin I . . . but I did not follow out my daydream, for the stranger brought me back to earth by inquiring what was my honest and unbiassed opinion of the Peruvians. I very cleverly pretended that I had swallowed some nicotine, and, after a polite pause for my answer, he went off to the subject of pearl fishing at Thursday Island. Then he looked at Dauvit's clock.

"Jerusalem!" he gasped, "the pub shuts at twa o'clock!" and he rushed out of the shop. I heaved a great sigh of relief, and then I heaved a greater sigh of relief.

I seized Dauvit by the arm.

"Dauvit," I gasped, "who—who is your cosmopolitan friend?"

"My what kind o' a friend?"

"Your world-travelled friend, Dauvit. Tell me who he is."

Dauvit laughed softly.

"That," he said, "was Joe Mill. He bides wi' his old mother in that cottage at the foot o' the brae. To the best o' my knowledge he hasna been further than Perth in his life."

"But!" I cried in amazement, "he has been everywhere!"

"He hasna," said Dauvit shortly, "but he works the cinema lantern at the Farfar picter hoose."

* * * * *

I had a long talk to-night with Macdonald about self-government in schools, and I told him of my plans for running a self-governing school in Highgate. At the end of the discussion I had the biggest surprise of my life. Mac smoked for a long time in silence, then he turned to me suddenly.

"Look here, old chap, I'll have a shot at introducing self-government to-morrow," he said with enthusiasm.

I grasped his hand.

"Excellent! Mac, you're a wonder! You're a brave man!"

"I don't feel brave," he said nervously. "It's going to be a very difficult job."

"It is," I said grimly, "and the most difficult part is for you to keep out of it."

"What do you mean?"

"I mean that you have been an authority for so long that you'll find yourself issuing orders unthinkingly. More than that the kiddies are so much dependent on you that they will wait to see how you vote."

"What's the best way to begin it?" he asked.

"Simply walk in to-morrow and say: 'Look here, you are going to govern yourselves. I have no power; I won't order anyone to do anything; I won't punish anyone. Now, do what you like'."

Mac looked frightened.

"But, good Lord, man, they'll—they'll wreck the school!"

"Funk!" I laughed.

His eyes were full of excitement.

"It'll be an awful job to keep my hands off them," he said half to himself.

"Funk!" I said again.

"It's all very well, but . . . well, I'm rather strict you know."

"So much the better! All the better a row!"

"You Bolshevist!" he laughed. He was like a boy divided between two desires—to steal the apples and to escape the policeman. I half feared that his courage would desert him.

"Here," he said, "why not come over to school?"

The temptation was great and I wavered.

"No," I said at last, "I can't do it. My presence would distract the children, and . . . they won't smash all the windows in front of a stranger. You want my support, you dodger!"

But I would give ten pounds to be in Mac's schoolroom to-morrow morning.

*   *   *   *   *

I went out this morning and sat on the school wall and smoked my pipe. I strained my ears for the first murmur of the approaching storm. Not a sound came from the schoolroom.

"Mac has funked it after all," I groaned, and went in to help Mrs. Macdonald to pare the potatoes.

When Mac came over at dinner-time his face wore a thoughtful look.

"You coward!" I cried.

"Coward!" he laughed. "Why, man, the scheme is in full swing!"

Then I asked him to tell me all about it.

"Your knowledge of children is all bunkum," he began. "You said there would be a row when I announced that I gave up authority."

"And wasn't there?"

"Not a vestige of one. The kids stared at me with open mouth, and . . ."

"And what?"

"Oh, they simply got out their books and began their reading lesson. As quiet as mice too."

"And do you mean to tell me that it made no difference?" I asked.

"None whatever. I tell you they just went on with the timetable as usual."

"But didn't they talk to each other more?"

"There wasn't a whisper."

I considered for a minute.

"What exactly did you say to them when you announced that they were to have self-government?"

"I just said what you told me last night."

"Did you add anything?"

He avoided my eye.

"Of course I said that I trusted them to carry on the school as usual," he admitted reluctantly.

"Thereby showing them that you didn't trust them at all," I explained. "Mac, you must have been a thundering strict disciplinarian. The kiddies are dead afraid of you. I fear that you'll never manage to have self-government. This fear of you must be broken, and you've got to break it."

"But how?" he asked helplessly.

"By coming down off your pedestal. You must become one of the gang. One dramatic exhibition will do it."

"What do you mean?"

"Smash a window; chuck books about the room . . . anything to break this idea that you are an exalted being whose eye is like God's always ready to see evil."

Mac looked annoyed and injured.

"What good will my fooling do?" he asked.

"But," I protested seriously, "it's essential. You simply must break your authority if you are to have a free school. There can be no real self-expression if you are always standing by to stamp out slacking and noise."

"But," he protested, "didn't I tell 'em I was giving up my authority?"

"Yes, but they don't believe you. You've got the eye of an authority."

He was by this time getting rather indignant.

"I can't go the length you do," he said sourly. "I'm not an anarchist."

"In that case I'd advise you to chuck the experiment, Mac," I said with an indifferent shrug of my shoulders. The shrug nettled Mac; he is one of the bull-dog breed, and I saw his lips set.

"I've begun it, and I won't chuck it," he said firmly. "And I hope to prove that your methods are all wrong. Let it come gradually; that's what I say."

When he came over at four o'clock his face glowed with excitement. He slapped me on the back with his heavy hand.

"Man," he cried, "it's going fine! We had our first trial this afternoon."

"Go on," I said.

"Oh, it was a first class start. Jim Inglis threw his pencil at Peter Mackie."

"I hope he didn't miss," I said flippantly.

Mac ignored my levity.

"And then I didn't know what to do. My first impulse was to haul him out and strap him, but of course I didn't. I just said to the class: 'You saw what Jim Inglis did? You have to decide what is to be done about it'."

"And they answered: 'Please, sir, give him the tawse'?" I said.

Mac laughed.

"That's exactly what they did say, but I told them that they were governing themselves, and suggested that they elect a chairman and decide by vote."

"Bad tactics," I commented. "You should have left them to settle their own procedure. What happened then?"

"They appointed Mary Wilson as chairman, and then John Smith got up and proposed that the prisoner get six scuds with the tawse from me. The motion was carried unanimously."

"You refused of course?" I said.

"Man, I couldn't refuse. I was alarmed, because six scuds are far too many for a little offence like chucking a pencil. I made them as light as possible."

I groaned.

"What would you have done?" he asked.

"Taken the prisoner's side," I said promptly, "I should have chucked every pencil in the room at the judge and jury. Then I should have pointed out that I refused to do the dirty work of the community."

"But where does the self-government come in there?" he protested. "Chucking things at the jury is anarchy, pure anarchy."

"I know," I said simply. "But then anarchy is necessary in your school. You don't mean to say that the children thought that throwing a pencil was a great crime? What happened was that they projected themselves on to you; unconsciously they said: 'The Mester thinks this a crime and he would punish it severely.' They were trying to please you. I say that anarchy is necessary if these children are to get free from their dependence on you and their fear of you. So long as you refuse to alter your old values you can't expect the kids to alter their old values. Unless you become as a little child you cannot enter the kingdom of—er—self-government."

I know that Mac's experiment will fail, and for this reason; he wants his children to run the school themselves, but to run it according to his ideas of government.

* * * * *

I think of an incident that happened when I was teaching in a school in London. I had a drawing lesson, and the children made so much noise that the teacher in the adjoining room came in and protested that she couldn't make her voice heard. The noise in my room seemed to increase . . . and the lady came in again. The noise increased.

Next day I went to my class.

"You made such a noise yesterday that the teacher next door had to stop teaching. She rightly complained. Now I want to ask you what you are going to do about it."

"You should keep us in order," said Findlay, a boy of eleven.

"I refuse," I said; "it isn't my job."

This raised a lively discussion; the majority seemed to agree with Findlay.

"Anyway," I said doggedly, "I refuse to be your policeman," and I sat down.

There was much talking, and then Joy got up.

"I think we ought to settle it by a meeting, and I propose Diana as chairman."

The idea was hailed with delight, and Diana was elected chairman and she took my desk seat and I went and sat down in her place.

Joy jumped up again.

"I propose that Mr. Neill be put out of the room."

The motion was carried.

"Righto!" I said, as I moved to the door, "I'll go up to the staff-room and have a smoke. Send for me if you want me."

I smoked a cigarette in the staff-room, and as I threw the stump into the grate Nancy came in.

"You can come down now."

I went down.

"Well," I said cheerily, "have you decided anything?"

"Yes," said the chairman, "we have decided that——"

Joy was on her feet at once.

"I propose that we don't tell Mr. Neill what we have decided. We can ask him at the end of the week if he notices any difference in our behaviour."

Others objected, and the matter was put to the vote. The voting was a draw, and Diana gave the casting vote in favour of my being told. Then she said that the meeting had agreed that if anyone made a row in class, he or she was to be sent to Coventry for a whole day.

"What will happen if I speak to the one that has been sent to Coventry?" asked Wolodia.

"We'll send you to Coventry too," said Diana, and the meeting murmured agreement.

No one was ever sent to Coventry, but I had no further complaints against the class. One interesting feature in the affair was this: Violet, a lively girl full of fun, one day got up and, as a joke, proposed that Mr. Neill be sent to Coventry. The others, usually willing to laugh with Violet, protested.

"That's just silly, Violet," they said. "If you propose silly things like that we'll send you to Coventry."

Then someone got up and proposed that Violet be sent to Coventry for being silly, and Diana at once took the chair. I got up and moved the negative, pointing out that I made no charge against her, and she was acquitted by a majority of one. I mention this to show that children of eleven and twelve can take their responsibilities seriously.

When I told the story to Macdonald he said: "But why didn't you join in their noise?"

"For two reasons, Mac," I said. "Firstly these children were not under the suppression of government schools; secondly it wasn't my school."

III.

The servant girl at the Manse has had an illegitimate child, and Meg Caddam, the out-worker at East Mains is cutting her dead. Thus the gossip of Mrs. Macdonald. Meg Caddam is the unmarried mother of three.

I have noticed again and again that the most severe critic of the unmarried mother is the unmarried mother, and I have many a time wondered at the fact. Now I know the explanation; it is the familiar Projection of a Reproach. Meg feels guilty because of her three children, but her guilt is repressed, driven down into the unconscious.

She dare not allow her conscious mind to face the truth, for then the truth would lower her self-respect; it would be unpleasant, out of harmony with her ego-ideal. But it is easy for her to project this inner reproach on to someone else, hence her blaming of the Manse lassie. Meg Caddam is really condemning herself, but she does not know it.

I used to despise the Meg Caddams as hypocrites, but, poor souls, they are not hypocrites. Their condemnation of their fallen sisters is genuine. It is wonderful how we all manage to divide our minds into compartments. Sandy Marshall of Brigs Farm is a most religious man, yet the other day he was fined for watering his milk. It is unjust to say that his religion is hypocritical. What happens is that his religion is shut up in one compartment of his mind, and his dishonesty is shut up in another compartment . . . and there is no direct communication between the compartments.

The mind is like one of the older railway carriages; education's task is to convert the old carriage into a new corridor carriage with communication between the compartments. Meg Caddam's own transgression against current morality is locked up in one compartment; her condemnation of the Manse girl is in another compartment. There is an unconscious communication, but there is no conscious communication. I don't know what Meg would say if a cruel friend pointed out to her that she also was a fallen woman.

I think that the gossip of this village mostly consists of projected reproaches. Liz Ramsay, an old maid and the super-gossip of Tarbonny, came into the schoolhouse this morning.

"Do ye ken this," she said to Mrs. Macdonald, "it's my opeenion that Mrs. Broon died o' neglect. I went to the door the day afore she died to speer hoo she was, and her daughter cam to the door, and do ye ken this? That lassie was smiling . . . *smilin'* . . . and her auld mother upstairs at death's door. Eh, Mrs. Macdonald, she's a heartless woman that Mary Broon. She killed her mother by neglect, that's what she did."

After she had gone I said to Mrs. Macdonald: "Who nursed Liz's mother when she died last June?"

"Nobody," said Mrs. Macdonald grimly. "Liz had too much gossip to retail in the village, and I'm told that Liz was seldom in the house."

I think I am guessing fairly rightly when I say that Liz feels guilty of neglecting her own mother, and like Meg Caddam she projects the reproach on to someone else.

* * * * *

Last Friday night I gave a lecture to the Literary Society in Tarby, our nearest town. I chose the subject of forgetting, and I told the audience of Freud and his great work in connection with the unconscious. To-day's *Tarby Herald* in reporting the lecture prints phonetically the spelling "Froid," but the *Tarby Observer* goes one better when it says: "Mr. Neill is an exponent of the new science of Cycloanalysis."

Which reminds me of a painful episode that took place when I was eighteen. I was much enamoured of a young university student, and I always strove to gain her favour by being interested in the things she liked. One day she informed me that she intended to take the Psychology class at St. Andrews the following session. I had never heard the word before, and I made a bold guess that it had something to do with cycles. In consequence we talked at cross purposes for a while.

"I'd love a subject like that," I said warmly.

"Most of it will be experimental psychology," she said.

My enthusiasm increased. I thought of the many experiments I had tried with my old cushion-tyred cycle.

"Excellent!" I cried. "A sort of training in inventing. Cranks, eh?" At that time my one ambition in life was to invent a folding crank that would give double power on hills.

The lady looked at me sharply.

"Why cranks?" she demanded. "I don't see it. Psychology has nothing to do with crystal-gazing you know."

I was gravelled.

"But what's the idea?" I asked. "Improvement of design?"

This made her think hard.

"H'm, yes, I think I know what you mean," she said slowly. "But remember that before you can improve the psyche you must know the psyche."

I hastened to agree.

"Certainly, but all the same there is much room for improvement. You don't want to come off at every hill, do you?"

This seemed to make her more thoughtful still.

"No," she said, "but don't you think that the mind makes the hill?"

This staggered me.

"Eh?" I gasped. "Mean to say that I broke my chain on Logie Brae yesterday because— —"

"I'm afraid it is too difficult for me," she said apologetically. "I get lost in metaphors."

Then I asked her something about ball bearings, and she threw me a grateful smile . . . for changing the subject—as she thought.

The most amusing joke is the joke about the innocent or ignorant. Everyone is tickled at the Hamlet joke I referred to in my *Log*.

The school inspector was dining with the local squire.

"Funny thing happened in the village school to-day," he said. "I was a little bit ratty, and I fired a question at a sleepy-looking boy at the bottom of the class.

"Here, boy, who wrote *Hamlet*?"

The little chap got very flustered.

"P—please, sir, it wasna me!"

The squire laughed boisterously.

"And I suppose the little devil had done if after all!" he cried.

We laugh at that story because we have all made mistakes owing to ignorance, and blushed for them a hundred times later. When we laugh at the squire, we are really laughing at ourselves; we are getting rid of our pent-up self-shame. That's why a good laugh is a medicine; it allows us to get rid of psychic poison, just as a good sweat rids us of somatic poison. Charlie Chaplin has possibly cured more people than all the psycho-analysts in the world.

* * * * *

Public speaking is a most difficult thing. It is difficult enough when you know your subject, and it is almost impossible if you don't. At a dinner someone asks you to get up and propose the health of the ladies. I tried proposing that toast once; luckily most of the diners were under the table by that time. What can one say about the ladies?

When you have a definite subject to talk about, and when you know everything about it, even then public speaking is difficult. You stand up before a sea of faces. You see no one; you dare not catch anyone's eye. The best plan is to fix your eye on the blurred face of the man at the back of the hall. You feel that the audience is vaguely hostile.

At one time I used to go straight into my subject . . . "Ladies and gentlemen, the subject of evolution has occupied the minds of—" Then the audience began to rustle, and the women turned to look at the hats behind them.

Nowadays I am more wary. I stand up and gaze over the sea of faces for a full minute. There is absolute silence. I put my hands into my trouser pockets and gaze at the ceiling, as if I were considering whether I should go on or give it up and go home. Even the boys at the back of the hall begin to look towards the platform.

Then I look down and find that my tie is hanging out of my waistcoat, and I adjust it. A girl of ten giggles.

"What can you expect for fivepence half-penny?" I ask, and the audience gasps.

"Why doesn't someone invent a long tie that won't come out at the ends?" I ask wearily, and there is a laugh. I go on from ties to collars, and there is another laugh. After that I can speak on education for two hours, and everyone in the hall will listen with great attention.

The first thing in public speaking is to get on good terms with your audience, and I claim that the best way to do this is to show them the human side of yourself. Some of your hearers are agin you; they have come out to criticise you. You disarm them at once by treating yourself as a joke. Of course you must suit your tactics to your audience. The tie remark will put me on good terms with a rural audience, but it would fail in a lecture to teachers in the Albert Hall.

An important thing to remember is that crowd humour is quite different from individual humour. A crowd will roar with delight if the lecturer accidentally knocks over the drinking glass on the table, but no individual ever laughs when a similar accident happens in a private room. Read the reports of speeches in the House of Commons. You will read that Lloyd George, in a speech, says: "And now let us turn to Ireland (loud laughter)." But in cold print it isn't a very good joke.

Quite a good way of commencing a lecture is to tell a short story . . . about the chairman if possible. But you must be careful. Keep off the topic of the chairman's marital affairs; he may have lodged a divorce petition the week before.

On second thoughts I think it better not to mention the chairman at all. Last winter the local mayor was presiding at a lecture I gave in an English town. After I had delivered the lecture, he got up.

"I came to this meeting feeling dead tired," he said, "but after Mr. Neill's lecture I feel as fresh as a daisy."

I rose in alarm.

"Ladies and gentlemen," I said hastily, "the mayor has been sitting behind me. Do tell me: has he been asleep?"

In the ante-room afterwards he assured me solemnly that he hadn't been asleep.

On Friday night I began thus: "Mr. Chairman, ladies and gentlemen, I am going to talk about Forgetting." Then I put my hand in my inside coat pocket; then I tried another pocket, and got very excited while I rummaged every pocket I had.

"I must apologise," I said, "but I have forgotten my notes."

The audience laughed, and we became the best of friends.

* * * * *

Forgetting is very often intentional. We forget what we do not want to remember. Brown writes to me saying that he is taking the wife and kids to the seaside, and would I please pay him the fiver I owe him? I at once sit down and write: "My dear Brown, I enclose a cheque for five quid. Many thanks for the loan. Hope you all have a good time at the sea."

Three days later Brown replies.

"Thanks for your letter, old man, but you forgot to enclose the cheque."

Why did I forget the cheque? Because I did not want to pay up. Consciously I did want to pay, for I wrote out the cheque all right, but my unconscious did not want to pay, and it was my unconscious that made me slip the cheque under the blotter.

Last summer I was invited to spend the week-end with some people at Stanmore. I did not want to go; a previous week-end with them had been most boring. However, I reluctantly consented to go out on the Saturday morning. When Saturday morning came I was not very much surprised to find that I had forgotten to put out my boots to be cleaned the night before.

"It looks as if I weren't keen on this trip," I said to myself.

I went down to Baker Street and got into the train. We stopped at many stations, and after an hour's journey I began to wonder what was wrong. I asked another man in the compartment when we were due at Stanmore, and he looked surprised.

"Why," he said, "you're on the wrong line; you ought to have changed at Harrow."

I got out at the next station and found that I had an hour to wait for the return train to Harrow. As I sat on the platform I took from my pocket my host's letter.

"Remember," it ran, "to change at Harrow," and the words were underlined.

I arrived four hours late . . . and spent a pleasant week-end.

One night I was dining out in London, and I told my host the new theory of forgetting.

"That's all bunkum," he said. "Why, there is a flower growing at the front door there, and I can never remember the name of it. I am fond of flowers and never have any difficulty in remembering their names as a rule."

"What flower is it?" I asked.

He tried to recall it, and had to give it up.

"It's the joke of the family," said his wife. "He can never remember the name Begonia."

"Begonia!" cried my host, "that's the name! But surely you don't mean to tell me that I want to forget it? Why should I?"

"It may be associated with something unpleasant in your life," I said.

"Nonsense!" he laughed. "The name conveys nothing to me."

We began to talk about other things. Ten minutes later my host suddenly exclaimed:

"I've got it!"

"What?" I asked.

"That Begonia business. When I began business as a chartered accountant over twenty years ago, the first books I had to audit were the books of a company calling itself The Begonia Furnishing Company. I glanced through the books and soon concluded that they were swindlers. I worried over that case for a week; you see it was my first case, and I felt a little superstitious about it. However, at the end of a week I sent the books back saying that I couldn't see my way to undertake the auditing. I've never given them a thought since."

I explained the mechanisms to him. The whole idea of this Begonia Company was so painful to him that he repressed it, that is, drove it down into the unconscious. Twenty years later he was unconsciously afraid to recall the name of the flower, because the name might have brought back the painful memories of the questionable books.

On Friday night during question time one man got up.

"Why is it, then," he asked, "that I cannot forget the painful time when my wife died?"

I explained that a big thing like that cannot be forgotten, but pointed out that in a case like that the tendency is to forget little things in connection with the big pain. I told him of a case I had myself known. A lady of my acquaintance lived for a few years in Glasgow; then she moved to Edinburgh, where she lived for almost thirty years. Now she lives in London. When she talks of her old home in Edinburgh she always says: "When we were in Glasgow." Invariably she makes this mistake. The reason is almost certainly this: just before she left Edinburgh she lost the one she loved most in life. She says: "When we were in Glasgow" because the word Edinburgh would at once bring back the painful memories connected with her loved one's death.

When I was teaching in Hampstead one of my pupils, a boy of sixteen, came to me one day.

"That's all rot, what you say about wanting to forget things," he said. "I went and left my walking-stick in a bus yesterday."

"Were you tired of it?" I asked.

"Tired of it?" he said indignantly. "Why, it was a beauty, a silver-topped cane, got it from mother on my birthday. That proves your theory is all wrong."

"Tell me about yesterday," I said.

"Well, I was going to a match at lord's, and it looked rather dull, so mother told me I'd better take a gamp. I said it wasn't going to rain, and took my cane, but

I had just got on the top of a bus when down came the rain in bucketfuls and I tell you I was wet to the skin."

"So you did mean to leave your cane behind?" I asked, with a smile.

"But I tell you I didn't!"

"You did, all the same. You kicked yourself because you hadn't taken your mother's advice and brought a gamp. You deliberately left your cane behind you because it had proved useless."

I must add that I failed to convince him.

Connected with forgetting are what Freud calls symptomatic acts. I leave my stick or gloves behind when I am calling at a house: I conclude that I want to go back there. I go to dinner at the Thomsons', and at their front door I absent-mindedly take out my latch-key. This may mean that I feel at home there; on the other hand, it may mean that I wish I were at home. It is dangerous to dogmatise about the unconscious.

I was sitting one night with Wilson, an old college friend of mine. We talked of old times, and I remarked that he had been very lucky in his lodgings during his college course.

"Yes," he said, "I was in the same digs all the five years. She was a ripping landlady was Mrs.—Mrs.—Good Lord! I've forgotten her name!"

He tried to recall the name, but had to give it up. Two hours later, as he rose to go, he exclaimed: "I remember the name now! Mrs. Watson!"

"What are your associations to the name Watson?" I asked.

"Associations? What do you mean?"

"What's the first thing that comes into your head in connection with the name?" I asked.

He made an effort to concentrate his mind, then suddenly he laughed shortly.

"Good Lord!" he cried, "that's my wife's name!"

I felt that I could not very well ask him anything further, but I suspected that Wilson and his wife were not getting on well together.

* * * * *

Macdonald's self-government scheme has fizzled out. Yesterday his scholars besought him to return to the old way of authority.

"They were fed up with looking after themselves," explained Mac to me. "They were always trying each other for misdemeanours, and they got sick of it."

I tried to explain to Mac why his attempt had failed. Self-government always fails unless it is complete self-government. Mac was the director and guide; it was he who decided the time-table; it was he who rang the bell and decided the length of the intervals. The children had nothing to do but to keep themselves in order, hence they came to spy on each other. All their energies were directed to penal measures. Their meeting degenerated into a police court. That was inevitable;

Mac, by laying down all the laws, prevented their using their creative energy on things and ideas. Naturally they put all the energy they had into the only thing open to them—the trial of offenders. In short, they were employing energy in destruction when they ought to have been employing it in construction. Mac seems indifferent now. "The thing is unworkable," he says.

* * * * *

Duncan came over to-night. I decided to let him do most of the talking, and he did it well. He has been doing a lot of Regional Geography, and I learned much from his conversation. As the evening wore on he became very affable, and he treated me with the greatest kindness. When Mac was seeing him out Duncan remarked to him: "That chap Neill isn't such a bad fellow after all." Now that I have shown Duncan that I am his inferior in Geography he will listen to me with less irritation.

After supper I went over to see Dauvit. His shop was crowded. Conversation was going slowly, and Dauvit seemed to welcome my entrance.

"Man, Dominie," he said, "I am very glad to see ye, cos the smith here has been tellin' his usual lees aboot the ten pund troot that he nearly landed in the Kernet."

"I doot ye dreamt it, smith," said the foreman from Hillend. "I ken for mysell that the biggest troot I ever catched were in my dreams."

"Dreams is just a curran blethers," said the smith in scorn.

Dauvit looked at him thoughtfully.

"That's a very ignorant remark, smith," he said gravely. "There's naebody kens what a dream is. Some o' thae spiritualist lads say that when ye are asleep yer spirit goes to the next plane, and that maks yer dreams."

The smith laughed loudly.

"Oh, Dauvit! Why, man, I dreamed last nicht that I was sittin' we a great muckle pint o' beer in my hand. Do ye mean to tell me that there is beer in heaven?"

There was a laugh at Dauvit's expense, but the laugh turned against the smith when Dauvit remarked dryly: "I didna mention heaven; I said the next plane, and onybody that kens you, smith, kens that the plane you're gaein' to is the doon plane."

"Naturally, a muckle pint o' beer will be the exact thing ye need doon there," he added.

"It's my opeenion," said old John Peters, "that dreams is just like a motor car withoot the driver. Or like a schule withoot the mester; the bairns just run aboot whaur they like, nae control as ye micht say. Weel, that's jest what happens in dreams; the mester is sleepin' and the bairns do all sorts o' mad things."

"Aye, man, John," said Dauvit, who seemed to be struck with the idea, "there's maybe something in that. Just as bairns when they get free do a' the things they're no meant to do, we do the same things in oor dreams. Goad, but I've done some awfu' things in my dreams!"

Here Jake Tosh the roadman began to cough, and Jake's cough always means that he is about to say something.

"You're just a lot o' haverin' craturs," he said with conviction. "If ye had ony sense ye wud ken that the dream is just cheese and tripe for supper."

Dauvit's eyes twinkled.

"And does the cheese wander frae yer stammick up to yer heid, Jake?"

"I wudna go so far as that," said Jake seriously, "but what I say is that a' the different parts o' the body work thegether. If the stammick has to work a' nicht to digest the cheese, the heid has to keep workin' at the same rate, and that's why ye dream."

"Aye, man, Jake," said Dauvit, "it's a bonny theory, but wud ye jest tell me exactly what work yer toes and fingers and hair are doin' a' nicht to keep upsides wi' yer stammick?"

Jake dismissed the question with an airy wave of his hand.

"Onybody kens that," he said; "they grow. Yer hair and yer nails grow at nichts, and that's why ye need a shave in the mornin'!"

"What if you don't dream at all, Jake?" I asked.

"Ye're needin' some grub," said Jake shortly.

On thinking it over I feel that Jake's theory throws some light on Jung's theory of the libido.

IV.

This morning I had a letter from a friend in London asking when I am going to set up my "Crank School" in London. I began to think about the word Crank. What is a Crank? Usually the name is applied to people who wear long hair, eat vegetarian diet, wear sandals . . . or something in that line. A Crank therefore is someone who differs from the crowd, and I am led to conclude that the Crank not only differs from the crowd but is usually ahead of the crowd.

According to Sir Martin Conway the crowd has no head; it can only feel. Hence it comes that the main feature of a crowd is its emotion. When we study the street crowd, the mob, this fact is evident; but can we say the same of other crowds . . . the Public School crowd, the Church, the Miners, the Doctors? I think so. The anger that Alec Waugh's book, *The Loom of Youth,* aroused in the public schools was not a thought-out anger; it came from the public school emotion. So with vivisection; the doctors' rage at the anti-vivisectionists is not an intellectual rage; it is simply a professional emotion. Just before I left London I happened one night to be in a company of men who were arguing about Re-incarnation. I had no special views on the subject, but I soon found myself supporting the crowd that was sceptical about Re-incarnation. The reason was that the leader of the anti-re-incarnation crowd happened to be a man called Neill. It is highly probable that if two rag-and-bone men got into a scrap in a public house they would support each other simply out of a professional crowd emotion.

That the crowd has no head is evident when we read the popular papers or see the popular films. The most successful papers are those that touch the passions of the mob. I proved this one week last spring. Judges were beginning to introduce the "cat" for criminals, as a means to stem the crime wave. I sat down and wrote an article on the subject, pointing out that this was a going back to the days of barbarism when lunatics were whipped behind the cart's tail. I made a strong plea for the psychological treatment of the criminal, basing my plea on the fact that crime is the result of unconscious workings of the mind, and stating that instead of sending a poor man to penal servitude we ought to analyse his mind and cure him of his anti-social tendencies.

I thought it a jolly good article, and when a prominent Sunday paper returned the manuscript to me I was surprised. My surprise left me on the following Sunday when the same paper blared forth an article by Horatio Bottomley. His title was: "Wanted—the Cat!"

My article was more thoughtful, more humane, more scientific. Why, then, was it suppressed? The answer is simple: it did not fit in with the passions of the crowd. It becomes clear why our best public men—editors, cabinet ministers, publicists are not great thinkers. They must keep in touch with the crowd; they must express the emotions of the crowd.

The attitude of the crowd to the anti-crowd person, the Crank, is never one of contemptuous indifference. It is always distinctly hostile. If I travel by tube from Hampstead to Piccadilly without a hat the other travellers stare at me with mild hostility. Why? Conway, in *The Crowd in Peace and War*, an excellent book, says that this hostility comes from fear. A crowd is always afraid of another crowd, because the only force that can destroy a crowd is a rival crowd. Every individual who differs from the herd is suspect because he is perhaps the nucleus of a rival crowd. That is why the world always crucifies its Christs.

The Crank School, then, is a school where anti-crowd people send their children. It is the school *par excellence* of the Intelligentsia. The tendency of every Crank School is to exaggerate the difference between the crank and the crowd; hence its adoption of an ideal and its concomitant crazes. I cannot for the life of me see why ideals are associated with vegetarianism, long hair, Grecian dress, and sandals, just as I cannot see why art should attach itself to huge bow-ties, long hair, and foot-long cigarette holders.

The Crank School holds up an ideal. It plasters its walls with busts of Walt Whitman and Blake; it hangs bad reproductions of Botticelli round the walls; it sings songs to Freedom; it rhapsodises about Beethoven and Bach. The children of the Crank Schools are, I rejoice to say, not cranks. They leave the boredom of Bach and seek the jazz record on the gramophone; they ignore the pictures of Whitman and Blake and study *The Picture Show* or *Funny Bits*. Many of them think more highly of Charlie Chaplin than of William Shakespeare.

I say again that I rejoice in this; it serves the Crank School people jolly well right. I cannot see by what right educators force what they consider good taste down the children's throats. That is a return to the old way of authority, of treating the child's mind as a blank slate. If the Crank Schools are to improve, they must drop their high moral purpose tone and come down to earth. They must realise that Charlie Chaplin and *John Bull* have their place in education just as Shakespeare and Beethoven have their place. We do not want to turn out cranks who will form a new superior crowd; we want to turn out men and women who will readily join the conventional crowd and help it to reach better ideals.

This question of good taste is a sore one with me. I think it fatal to impose good taste on any child; the child must form his own taste. I know that it is possible to cultivate good taste and to become a very superior cultivated person, but I know that the human, erring, vulgar, music-hall, Charlie Chaplin part of such a person's make-up is not annihilated; it is merely repressed into the unconscious.

I have a theory that each of us has a definite amount of human nature, some of it high, some of it low, or, to phrase it differently, some of it animal, some of it spiritual. We can repress one part, and then we become either a saint or a sinner; the better way is to be both saint and sinner, to look life straight in the face, condemning no one, judging no one.

* * * * *

Macdonald was re-reading *A Dominie Dismissed* to-night, and he looked up and said: "Look here, you've got an awful lot of swear-words in this book!"

"That," I said, "has a cause, Mac. They aren't really swear-words; the world has grown out of being shocked at a 'damn,' but I am willing to admit that there are more damns and hells than is usual. They are symptomatic; they date back to my early days when swearing was a crime punishable with the strap. They are simply symbols of my freedom. Most bad language is from a like cause. When you foozle on the first tee there is no earthy reason why you should say 'Hell' rather than 'Onions'! But if onions had been taboo when you were a child you would find yourself using the word as a swear. The curse word is the link that joins your foozle with the nursery; whenever you curse you regress, that is, you go back to the infantile."

"But," said Mac, "you don't mean to say that if swearing were permitted to children that they wouldn't curse when they were grown up?"

"I don't think they would," I said. "Nor would there be any unprintable stories if we had a frank sex education. It's a sad fact, Mac, but nine-tenths of humour is due to early suppression and repression."

"Seems to me," said Mac with a laugh, "that if everybody were psycho-analysed, the world would be a pretty dull place."

* * * * *

A few days ago I found a pot of light paint in Mac's workshop, and, impelled by heaven only knows what unconscious process, I painted my bicycle blue. This morning, the paint being dry, I rode forth into an unsympathetic world. Women came to their doors to stare at my machine, and as they stared they broke into laughter. When I reached the village of Cordyke the school was coming out, and I was greeted with a howl of derision. I thought it a good instance of crowd psychology; I was different from the crowd, and I evoked laughter and derision.

After cycling a few miles, I came to an old man breaking stones at the bottom of a hill. On my approaching he threw down his hammer and turned to stare at my cycle. I dismounted.

"Almichty me!" he said with surprise. "That's a michty colour!"

"It's unusual," I said, as I lit a cigarette.

He fumbled for his clay pipe.

"I've seen black anes, and I wance saw a silver-plated ane, but I never heard tell o' a blue bike afore," he said. "Did you pent it?"

I acknowledged that it was my very own handiwork.

"But," he said in puzzled tones, "what was yer idea?" and he stared at it again. "A michty colour that!"

I threw my bike down on the grass and sat down on the cairn.

"Between you and me," I said mysteriously, "I had to paint it blue."

He raised his eyebrows.

"Yea, man!"

"Government orders," I said carelessly, and began to throw stones at a tree trunk at the other side of the road.

"Government orders?" He looked very much surprised.

"Yes," I said airily. "You see, it's like this. The Coalition Government isn't very firmly placed these days, and, well, I'm an agent for it. Of course, you know that it is really a Tory government, and my bike, as it were, invites the electorate to vote True Blue."

"Yea, man! I thocht that you was maybe ane o' thae temperance lads frae Americky."

"Ah!" I said solemnly, "that reminds me; Pussyfoot tried to induce me to make my tour a sort of joint thing. He suggested that I might carry on my Tory work, and at the same time take part in the blue ribbon campaign. Of course I refused."

"Of coorse," he nodded.

"Officially I am doing Coalition work," I continued conversationally, "but I have motives of my own."

"You don't say!"

"Oh, yes. I am a great admirer of Lord Fisher and the Blue Water school, sometimes spoken of as the Blue Funk school. Again, I find that the Great War has left many people in the blues, and by means of homeopathy I cure 'em; I mean to say that they come to their doors and laugh at my blue bike. My blue dispels their blues."

The old man did not seem to follow this.

"Of course," I went on, "the Bluebells of Scotland have something to do with my selection of the colour."

"A verra nice sang," he commented.

"An excellent song! Then there is the well-known phrase 'Once in a Blue Moon,' and innumerable songs about the pale moonlight. Also I once knew a man who had the blue devils."

I tried to think of other phases of blueness, but my stock was almost exhausted.

"Of course," I added, "I am not forgetting the other blues, the Oxford blues, Reckitt's Blue, Blue Coupons, and—and—I'm afraid I can't think of any other blues just at the moment."

The old man drew the back of his hand over his mouth.

"There's the 'Blue Bonnets' up at the tap o' the brae," he suggested thirstily.

"Good idea!" I cried, "come on!" and together we climbed the brae.

* * * * *

A friend of mine in London has written me asking if I will write an article on Co-education for an educational journal, in which she is interested. I replied: "I can't see where the problem comes in; to a Scot co-education is not a thing that has to be supported by argument; he accepts it as he accepts the law of gravitation."

I wonder why English people are so afraid of co-education. To this day schools like Bedales, King Alfred's, Harpenden, and Arundale are reckoned as crank schools. The great middle-class of England believes in segregation. Even Dr. Ernest Jones, the most prominent Freudian psycho-analyst in England, appears to be afraid of it.

I can only conjecture that Jones agrees with the middle and upper classes in associating sex with sin. I have never tried to think out my reasons for believing in co-education; possibly the true reason is that having grown up in a co-education atmosphere, co-education has become a part of me just as my Scots accent has. In other words, I may have a co-education complex. If that is so, my arguments will be mere rationalisations, but I give them for what they are worth.

We are all born with a strong sex instinct, and this instinct must find expression in some way. We know that the sex energy can be sublimated, that is, raised to a higher power. For instance, the creative sex urge may be directed to the making of a bookcase, or the making of a century at cricket. But I know of no evidence to prove that all the instinct can be sublimated. An adolescent may spend his days at craftwork and games, but he will have erotic dreams at nights. All the drawing and painting in the world will not prevent his having emotion when he looks at the face of a pretty girl.

In our segregation schools boys and girls see nothing of each other. The unsublimated sex instinct finds expression in homosexuality, that is the emotion that should go to the opposite sex is fixed on a person of the same sex. I admit that we are all more or less homosexual; otherwise there could be no friendship between man and man, or woman and woman. In our boarding schools the sex instinct often takes the road of auto-eroticism.

In a co-education school the sex impulse is directed to one of the opposite sex. This attachment is nearly always a romantic ideal attachment. I have never known a case that went the length of kissing; among little children at a rural school, yes; at the age of seven I kissed my first sweetheart; but among adolescents I find that neither the boy nor the girl has the courage to kiss. Theirs is a sublimated courtship; they never use the word Love; they talk about "liking So-and-so."

That at many co-education schools this romantic attachment is more or less an underground affair is due to the moral attitude of teachers. They pride themselves on the beautiful sexless attachments of their pupils; they give moral lectures on the subject of kissing, and naturally every pupil in school at once becomes painfully self-conscious on the subject. The truth is that many co-educationists do not in their hearts believe in the system; they still see sin in sex.

To be a thorough success the co-education school must include sex education in its curriculum. The children of the most advanced parents seldom get it at home, and they come to school with the old attitude to sex. Sex education does not mean telling children where babies come from; it should dwell mostly on the psychological side of the question. The child ought to learn the truth about its sex instinct. Most important of all, the child who has indulged in auto-eroticism ought to be helped to get rid of his or her sense of guilt. This sense of guilt is the primary evil of self-abuse; abolish it, and the child is on the way to a self-cure.

How many children can go to their teacher and make confession of sex troubles? Very few. It is the teachers' fault; they set themselves up as moralists, and a moralist is a positive danger to any child.

Not long ago I was addressing a meeting of teachers in south London. At question time a woman challenged me.

"You have condemned moralists," she said; "do you mean to say that you would never teach a child the difference between right and wrong?"

"Never," I answered, "for I do not know what is right and what is wrong."

"Then I think you ought not to be a teacher," she said.

"I know what is right for me, and wrong for me," I went on to explain, "but I do not know what is right and wrong for you. Nor do I presume to know what is right or wrong for a child."

I was pleasingly surprised to find that the meeting roared approval of my reply.

* * * * *

Macdonald had to attend a funeral to-day, and he asked me if I would take his classes for an hour. I gladly agreed.

"Give them a lesson on psychology," he said; "it will maybe improve their behaviour."

I went over to the school at two o'clock, and Mac introduced me, although I had already made friends with most of the children in the playground and the fields. Mac then went away and I sat down at his desk.

"We'll have a talk," I said, "just a little friendly talk between you and me. I want to hear your opinions on some things."

They looked at me with interest.

"Why," I said, "why do you sit quiet in school?"

Andrew Smith put up his hand.

"Please, sir, 'cause if we don't the mester gies us the strap."

"A very sound reason, too," I commented. "And now I want to ask you why you sometimes want to throw papers or slate-pencils about the room."

"Please, sir, we never do that," said little Jeannie Simpson.

"The mester wud punish us," said another girl.

"But," I cried, "surely one of you has thrown things about the room?"

Tom Murray, the bad boy of the school (according to Mac), put up his hand.

"Please, sir, I did it once, but the mester licked me."

"Why did you do it, Tom?"

Tom thought hard.

"I didna like the lesson," he said simply.

I then went on further.

"Now I want you all to think this out: was Tom being selfish when he threw paper, or was he unselfish?"

Everyone, Tom included, judged that the paper-throwing was a selfish act.

"I don't agree," I said. "Tom was trying to do a service to the others; you were all bored by a lesson, and Tom stepped in and took your attention. Unfortunately he also attracted the attention of Mr. Macdonald, but that has nothing to do with Tom's reason for doing it. Tom was the most unselfish of the lot of you; he showed more good than any of you."

"The mester didna think that!" said Tom, with a grin.

Peter Wallace carefully rolled a paper pellet and threw it at Tom.

"Now," I said with a smile, "let's think this out; why did Peter throw that pellet just now?"

"Because the class is bored," said a little girl, and there was a good laugh at my expense.

"Righto!" I laughed, "shall we do something else?" but the class shouted "No!" and I proceeded.

"Peter, do tell us why you threw that pellet."

"For fun," said Peter, blushing and smiling.

"He did it so's the class wud look at him," said Tom Murray, and Peter hid his diminished head.

"A wise answer, Tom," I said; "but we are all like that; we all like to be looked at. Who is the best at arithmetic?"

"Willie Broon," said the class, and Willie Broon cocked his head proudly.

"And who is the best fighter?"

"Tom Murray," answered the boys, and one little chap added: "Tom cud fecht Willie Broon wi' one hand."

Tom tried to look modest.

I went round the class and with one exception every child had at least one branch of life in which he or she found a sense of superiority. The exception was Geordie Wylie, a small lad of thirteen with a white face and a starved appearance. The class were unanimous in declaring that Geordie had no talent.

"He canna even spit far enough," said one boy.

Geordie's embarrassment made me change the subject quickly, but I made up my mind to have a talk with him later.

Some of the reasons for individual pride were strange. Jake Tosh's feeling of superiority lay in the circumstance that his father had laid out a gamekeeper while poaching. Jock Wilson had once found a shilling; another boy had seen "fower swine stickit a' in wan day;" another could smoke a pipe of Bogie Roll without sickening (but I had to promise not to tell the Mester). The girls seemed to find their superiority mostly in lessons, although a few were proud of their needle-work.

I then went on to ask them what their highest ambition in life was. The boys showed less imagination than the girls. Six of them wanted to be ploughmen like their fathers. To a townsman this might appear to be a very modest ambition, but to a boy it means power and position; to drive a pair of horses tandem fashion as they do on the East Coast, with the tracer prancing on the braes; that is what being a ploughman means to a village lad. One boy wanted to be an engineer, another a clerk ("'cos he doesna need to tak' aff his jaicket to work!"), another a soldier.

"Not a single teacher!" I said.

"We're no clever enough," said Tom Murray.

I turned to the girls.

"Now, let's see what ambition you have," I said hopefully. The result was good; three teachers, two nurses, one typist, one lady doctor, one . . . lady. This was Maggie Clark. She just wanted to be like one of thae ladies in the picters with a motor car.

"And husband?" I asked.

"No, I dinna want a man, but I wud like a lot of bairns," she said, and there was a snigger from the boys who had got their sex education from the ploughmen at the Brig of evenings.

Another girl remarked that Maggie's ambition was a selfish one.

"But are you not all selfish?" I asked.

The class indignantly denied it.

"Right," I said, "what do you say to a composition exercise?"

They obediently got out their composition books, but I told them that my exercise was an easy one. I tore up a few pages into slips and distributed them.

"Now," I said, "suppose I give you five pounds to do what you like with. Write down what you would do with it, fold the paper, and hand it in to me."

They eagerly agreed, and at the end of five minutes I had a hatful of slips. I then drew a line down the centre of the blackboard. On one side I wrote the word Selfish; on the other Unselfish. The class groaned and laughed.

"Now," I said cheerfully, "this will prove whether the class is unselfish or not," and I unfolded the first slip.

"But you'll say we are selfish!" said a boy.

"I have nothing to do with it," I said; "you are to decide by vote. First person . . . 'I would buy a bicycle': selfish or unselfish?"

"Selfish!" roared the class, and I put a mark in the first column.

"Next paper . . . 'Scooter, knife, and the rest on ice-cream.'"

"Selfish!" and I put down another mark.

"Next: . . . 'Buy a pair of boots' . . . selfish or unselfish?"

The class had to stop and think here.

"Selfish!" said a few.

"Unselfish," said others, "'cos he wud be helpin' his mother."

"Then we'll vote on it," I said, and by a majority of two the act was declared to be unselfish.

We then had a run of knives, tops, candy, cycles, and no vote was necessary. Then came a puzzler.

"I would send every penny to the starving babies of Germany."

"Unselfish!" cried the class in one voice. I was just about to put the mark in the unselfish column when a boy said: "That's selfish, cos she'd feel proud of being so—so unselfish."

"How do you know it is a she?" I asked.

"'Cause I ken it's Jean Wilson," he answered promptly; "she has took a reid face."

There followed a breezy debate on Jean's act.

"It is selfish," said Mary, "because when you do a kind action you feel pleased with yourself, and it was selfish because if it hadna pleased her she wud never ha' done it."

I asked for a vote and to my astonishment the act was declared selfish by a majority of three. I suspect that conventional Hun Hatred had something to do with the voting.

The voting over I totted up the marks.

"You have judged yourselves," I said, "and according to your own showing you as a class are 87 per cent. selfish and 13 per cent. unselfish."

This essay in composition was not original; I got the idea from Homer Lane, who claimed that it was the best introduction to school psychology. "It is the best way to make children think of their own behaviour," he said, and my experiment has shown this.

When Mac came back I said to him; "You've got a fine lot of bairns, Mac."

"Had you any difficulty?" he asked.

"What do you mean?"

"Oh, I half thought they would try to pull your leg, especially a boy like Tom Murray. He is a most difficult chap, you know."

"Tom's a saint," I said; "every child is a saint if you treat him as an equal. No, I had no difficulty, but I want you to send over Geordie Wylie to me this afternoon. There is something wrong with that boy; he has no ambition and he has one of the worst inferiority complexes I have ever struck. I want to have a quiet talk with him."

Mac promised, and at three o'clock Geordie came over to the schoolhouse. I took him into the parlour, and he sat nervously on the edge of a chair.

"Tell me about yourself, Geordie," I said, but he did not answer.

"Do you keep rabbits?"

"Aye."

"What kind?"

"Twa Himalayas and a half Patty."

"Keep doos?"

"No."

It was like drawing blood from a milestone.

"What do you do when you go home at nights?"

It was a long difficult task to get anything out of him. The only fact of value I got was that he was a great reader of Wild West stories. I asked him to come to me again, and he said he would.

To-night I asked Mac about him.

"He's a dreamer," said Mac, "and he's lazy. I am always strapping him for inattention. He's not a manly boy, never plays games, always stands in a corner of the playground."

"Does he ever fight?" I asked.

"He's a great coward, but there's one queer thing about him; when any boy challenges him to fight he goes white about the gills but he always fights . . . and gets licked."

"Mac," I said, "will you do me a favour? Don't whack him again; it is the worst treatment you can give him. He is a poor wee chap, and he is badly in need of real help."

"All right," said the kindly Mac, "I'll try not to touch him, but he irritates me many a time."

* * * * *

I had Geordie for an hour this morning. He was taciturn at first, but later he talked freely. He is very much afraid of his father, and he weeps when his father scolds him. This makes the father angrier and he calls Geordie a lassie, a greetin' lassie. This jeer wounds the boy deeply. He is afraid in the dark. He told me that he was puzzled about one thing; when he goes for his milk at night he is never afraid on the outward journey, but when he leaves the dairy to come home he is always in terror. I asked him what he was afraid of and he told me that he always imagined that there was a man in a cheese-cutter cap waiting to murder him.

"What is a cheese-cutter?" I asked.

"It is a bonnet with a big snout, something like a railway porter's. My father's a porter and he has ane."

Evidently the man he is afraid of is his father. This may account for his lack of fear when he is walking from his home to the dairy. Then he is leaving his father; when he starts to return he is going back to his father and is afraid.

I asked him about his fights with other boys. He always feared a fight but he went through with it so that the other boys should not call him a coward. Naturally he always lost the battle; he fought with a divided mind; while his less imaginative opponent thought only of hitting and winning, Geordie was picturing the end of the fight.

I asked him if he had a sweetheart, and he blushed deeply. He told me that he often took fancies for girls, but they would not have him. Frank Murray always cut him out; Frank was a big hefty lad and the girls like the beefy manly boy.

He does much day-dreaming, phantasying it is called in analysis. His dreams always take the form of conquests; in his day-dream he is the best fighter in the school, the best scholar, the most loved of the girls. His night dreams are often terrifying, and he has more than once dreamt that his father and Macdonald were dead. He finds compensation for his weaknesses in his day-dreams and his reading. He likes tales of heroes who always kill the villians and carry off the heroines.

It is difficult to know what to do in a case like this. The best way would be to change the boy's environment, but that is out of the question. Even then the early fears would go with him; he would transfer his father-complex to another man.

I tried to explain to Mac the condition of Geordie. The boy is all bottled up; his energy should be going into play and work, but instead it is regressing, going back to early ways of adaptation to environment.

"But what can I do with him?" asked Mac.

"Give him your love," I said. "He fears you now, and your attitude to him makes him worse. You must never punish him again, Mac."

"That's all very well," said Mac ruefully, "but what am I to do? Suppose Tom Murray and he talk during a lesson, am I to whack Tom and allow Geordie to get off?"

"Chuck punishment altogether," I said. "You don't need it; it is always the resort of a weak teacher."

"I couldn't do without it," he said.

"All right then," I said wearily, "but I want you to realise that your punishments are making Geordie a cripple for life."

* * * * *

I went down and had a talk with Geordie's father. He was not very pleasant about it; indeed he was almost unpleasant.

"There's nothing wrong wi' the laddie," he said aggressively. "He's a wee bit lassie-like and he has no pluck."

Here Geordie entered the kitchen, and his father turned on him harshly.

"Started to yer lessons yet?" he demanded.

Geordie muttered something about having had to feed his rabbits.

"I'll rabbit ye! Get yer books oot this minute!" and Geordie crept to a corner and rummaged among some old clothes for his school-bag.

I tried to be as amiable as I could, and avoided controversy. I soon saw that father and mother were not pulling well together, and I suspected that the father's harshness to Geordie was often a weapon to wound the fond mother. I saw that nothing I could say would do any good, and I took my departure.

Later I went to see Dauvit, and found him alone. I asked him to tell me about the Wylies.

"Tam Wylie is wan o' the stupidest men in a ten mile radius," said Dauvit. "But he's no stupid whaur money is concerned; they tell me that he drinks aboot half his week's wages, and his puir wife has to suffer. That laddie o' theirs, he was born afore the marriage, and they tell me that Tam wud never ha' married her if he hadna been fell drunk the nicht he put in the banns."

This case of poor Geordie shows what a complexity there is in human affairs. His father has a mental conflict, and he drinks so that he may get away from reality. The father's drinking and the son's reading of romances are fundamentally the same thing; each is trying to get away from a reality he dare not face. No treatment of Geordie could be satisfactory unless at the same time the parents were being treated.

V.

Carrotty Broon, one of my old scholars, came to Dauvit's shop to-night, and he talked about his pigeons . . . his doos he calls them. He keeps a pigeon loft of homers, and he spends a considerable amount in training them.

"Some fowk think," he said, "that a homer will flee hame if ye throw it up five hunder miles awa."

"I've read of flights of seven hundred miles," I said.

Carrotty Broon chuckled.

"I mind o' a homer I had," he went on. "He was a beauty, a reid chequer. His father had flown frae London to Glasgow, and his mither was a flier too. Weel, I took him doon to Monibreck on my bike, and let him off. I never saw him again; five mile, and he cudna find his way hame!"

"He must ha' been shot," said Dauvit, "for thae homers find their way hame by instinct."

"Na, na, Dauvit," said Broon, "they flee by sicht. When ye train a homer ye tak it a mile the first day, syne three miles, syne maybe seven, ten, twenty, fifty, and so on. Send the purest bred homer fower mile without trainin' and ye'll never see him again."

Carrotty Broon told us many interesting things about doos and their ways. We listened to him because he was an authority and we knew little about the subject.

"The only thing I ken aboot doos," said Dauvit with a laugh, "is that when I was a laddie auld Peter Smith and John Wylie keepit homers and they were aye trying compeetitions in fleein'. John was gaein' to London for his summer holiday, and so him and Peter made a bargain that they wud flee twa homers from London. Weel, John he got to London, and he thocht to himsell that seein' they had a bet o' twa pund on the race, he wud mak sure o' winnin', and so what does he do but tak a pair o' shears and cut the wing o' Peter's doo.

"When John cam hame after a fortnight's trip he met auld Peter at the station.

"'Weel, Peter,' says he, 'wha won the race?'

"'You,' said Peter; 'your doo cam hame the next day, but mine only got hame this mornin'. And it has corns on its feet like tatties.'"

* * * * *

To-day was Macdonald's Inspection Day, and at dinner time he brought over Mr. J. F. Mackenzie, H.M.I.S., a middle-aged man and Mr. L. P. Smart, assistant

I.S., a cheery youth fresh from Oxford. When inspectors dine with the village dominie they never mention the word education. These two talked a lot, and all their conversation was about mountain-climbing in Switzerland. They swopped long prosy yarns about dull incidents, and I was very much bored. So was Mac, but he pretended to be interested, but then he was to see them again, and I wasn't . . . at least I prayed that I might not. After a time I began to feel that I was being left out of the conversation, and I waited until Mackenzie paused for a breath.

"Switzerland is very beautiful," I remarked, "but you should see the Andes."

Mackenzie looked at me coldly.

"I haven't been to South America," he said.

"Same here," said I cheerfully, "but I remember seeing pictures of them in the geography book at school."

Mackenzie looked at me more coldly than before. I don't think he liked me, and when the younger man chuckled Mackenzie glared at him. Smart had a sense of humour.

"I'm afraid we have been boring you," he said to me with a smile.

"I'd rather listen to you two talking education," I confessed.

Mackenzie waved the suggestion away.

"I leave education behind when I walk out of the school," he said in grand manner. "Most excellent rhubarb, Mrs. Macdonald. Home grown?" And then we had ten minutes of garden products versus shop greens. I admit that this inspector had a genius for small talk. We dismissed greens and I led the conversation to hens and ducks. Mackenzie did not know much about them, and he confirmed my opinion of his genius for small talk by saying: "Buff Orpingtons! They are named after Orpington in Kent. I remember staying a night there before I went to Switzerland . . ." and the dirty dog took the conversation back to his mountain climbing.

I made a gesture to the younger man and got him out into the garden.

"Why does he waste precious time talking about cabbages and dreary Swiss inns?" I asked.

Smart laughed shortly.

"You know how rich folk talk at table when the servants are present?"

I nodded.

"Well, that's the Chief's attitude to teachers; he never says anything of any importance whatever."

"But why?"

"He is of the old school. He has been inspecting schools for forty years. In the olden days an inspector was a sort of Almighty; teachers quaked before him because with a stroke of his pen he could reduce their money grant. To this day the old man treats teachers as a king treats his subjects—with kindness but with distance."

"Has he any views on education?" I asked.

Smart shook his head.

"None, but he has heaps of views on instruction and discipline. By the way, he thinks that Macdonald's discipline is very good."

"And you?"

"I think it rotten," he said ruefully, "but what can I do? A junior inspector is a nobody; if he has any views of his own he has to pocket them. I would chuck out all this discipline rot and go in for the Montessori stunt. Take my tip and never accept an inspectorship."

"I won't," I said hastily.

I liked Smart, and I wish we had more of his stamp in the inspectorate.

When we returned to the dining-room Mackenzie looked at me with interest.

"I didn't know that you were the *Dominie's Log* man till Mr. Macdonald told me two minutes ago," he said. "I am delighted to meet you. I enjoyed your book very much indeed. Very amusing."

He was quite affable now. Writing a book gives a man a certain standing. I fancy it is the dignity of print that does it, and we all have the print superstition. I find myself accepting statements in books, whereas if someone said the same things to me over a dinner-table I should refute them with scorn. "If it is in *John Bull* it is so!" Mr. Bottomley is a sound psychologist.

When they were departing I said to Smart: "Yes, he's very amiable and all that, but I am jolly glad I had Frank Michie and not him as my chief inspector when I wrote my *Log*."

Smart laughed.

"My dear chap, Mackenzie would have let you run your school in your own way."

"But," I cried, "he doesn't believe in freedom!"

"He doesn't, but don't you see that he simply couldn't have jumped on you? He would have thought you either a lunatic or a genius, and he would have feared to condemn you in case you might turn out to be the latter. I know an art critic in London, and, believe me, the poor devil lives in terror lest he should damn the work of a new Augustus John. The Futurists aren't flourishing on their merits; they are flourishing because the critics are in a holy funk to condemn them in case they might be artists after all."

I want to meet Smart again. I like his style.

* * * * *

I am indeed a Dominie in Doubt. What is education striving after? I cannot say, for education is life and what the aim of life is no one knows. Psycho-analysis can clear up a life; it can release bottled up energy, but it cannot say how the released energy is to be used. The analyst cannot advise, because no man can tell another how to live his life. Freud clears up the past, but he cannot clear up the future.

Is there such a thing as Re-incarnation? I wonder. Am I living the life that my past lives on earth fitted me for? If so analysis is wrong. If I am suffering from a severe neurosis it is because I earned this punishment in my past lives, and Freud has no right to cure me. He is interfering with the plans of the Almighty. If, as I have heard a Theosophist declare, the children in the slums are miserable because they failed to learn their lesson in previous lives, then the people who try to abolish slums are all wrong. I think my Theosophist would argue that the charitable person is growing in grace, thereby rising above his previous lives. And thus one soul helps another to rise to perfection. It may be, and I hope it is so, for then life would have a meaning. Pain and war would then be less terrible, for they would be but incidents in the eternal unfolding of perfection.

Yet I find myself doubting. If I am William Shakespeare born again I do not know it, and I am left in doubt as to whether I may not have been Charles Peace instead. Possibly I was both.

Then there is psychical research. I have been to a medium and have heard things that all the psycho-analysis in the world cannot account for. I want to believe that the dead can speak to us, but where are the dead? I have read Sir Oliver Lodge's *Raymond*, and the description of the next world given there. Frankly I don't fancy it, and I have no desire to go there.

How then can I attempt to educate children when the ultimate solution of life is denied me? I can only stand by and give them freedom to unfold. I do not know whither they are going, but that is all the more a reason why I ought not to try to guide their footsteps. This is the final argument for the abolition of authority. We may beat and break a horse because we selfishly require a horse's service, and according to the accepted view a horse has no immortal soul. We dare not beat and break a child, for a child is going to an end that we cannot know.

I like the Theosophist schools, although I do not like all Theosophists. Some of them seem to be living the higher life consciously, and repressing their lower natures. Most of them do not smoke or drink or eat meat or swear or go to music-halls. That may be living on a higher plane, but it is not living fully. Still, in many ways they are broad-minded. In their schools they do not force Theosophy down the children's throats; they allow a great amount of freedom, but their schools are not free schools. There is a definite attempt to mould character chiefly by insisting on good taste. I am quite sure that no head-master of a Theosophical School would take his children to see a Charlie Chaplin film. Charlie is not obviously living the higher life; he stands for the vulgar side of life; he picks up girls and gets drunk (in the play) and is sea-sick and very vulgar about soda-water.

I find myself insisting on the inclusion of Charlie in any scheme of education because no one ought to be taught to be shocked at sea-sickness and soda-water squirting. Charlie to me is the antidote to the higher-plane crowd; he and his kind are as essential as Shelley. I admit that reading Shelley is a higher kind of pleasure than watching "Champion Charlie," but no human being can safely live on the higher plane, and no child wants to. Education must deal with *all* life; a higher plane diet will produce hot-house plants, beautiful perhaps, but delicate and artificial.

* * * * *

Old Willie Murray the cobbler had been bed-ridden for over a year, and when I dropped into Dauvit's shop this morning Mary Rickart was telling Dauvit that his old master was dead.

"Aye, Dauvit," she was saying when I entered, "I'm no the kind that speaks ill o' the deid, but I will say this, that Wull Murray had his faults. Aye, and though he's a corp the day, I canna pertend that he was ony freend o' mine."

When Mary had gone Dauvit turned to me with a queer smile.

"Dominie, you tell me that you have studied the science o' the mind, psy—what is't you call it?"

"Psychology," I said.

"That's the word. Weel then, dominie, just tell me why Mary Rickart had sic a pick at auld Willie Murray."

I smoked for a time thoughtfully.

"It's difficult, Dauvit. I haven't got enough evidence. However I think I can make a good guess."

"Weel?"

"Mary and Willie sat in the same class at school?"

"Good!" said Dauvit, "they did."

"And Mary was Willie's first sweetheart?"

"Imphm!"

"Mary loved Willie and he loved her. They were sweethearts for a long time, but another damsel came and stole Willie's heart away. Mary wept bitter tears, but in time she repressed her love . . . and it changed into hate."

Dauvit chuckled.

"A very nice story," he said, "but, ye ken, it's just a story. You cudna guess the real reason why Mary hated him so much."

"Then what was the real reason, Dauvit?"

He laughed.

"Mary hated Willie Murray because he aince telt her that she was a silly woman to think that she cud wear a number fower shoe on a number acht foot."

We laughed together, and then I said:

"Dauvit, why did you never marry? You like women I fancy."

My remark made him thoughtful.

"Man," he said, "I've often speered the same question o' mysel. As a young man I was gye fond o' the lassies, but . . . I dinna ken!" and he broke off suddenly and took up a boot. "Thae soles are just paper noo-a-days," he growled.

I refused to let him run away from the subject.

"Had you a sweetheart?" I asked.

He laughed boisterously to hide his confusion.

"Dozens o' them!" he cried.

"Then why didn't you marry one of them?"

He shook his head.

"Dominie, that's the question." He stared at the grate for a while. "There was Maggie Adams, a bonny lassie she was. Man, I mind when I took her to Kirriemair Market . . ." He sighed. "Aye, man, dominie, I liked Maggie mair than ony o' the others."

"Did she love someone else?" I asked softly.

Dauvit took some time to reply.

"No, man, Maggie wanted me."

"Then the fault lay on your side? You didn't love her!"

Dauvit brought his hand down on the board.

"Goad, man, but I did!"

I could not understand.

"Man, on the road hame frae Kirrie Market I was to speer if she wud marry me . . . but I didna."

We smoked silently for a long minute.

"Ye see," he went on slowly, "Maggie was a bonny lassie and I liked to kiss and cuddle her, but kissin' and cuddlin' are a very sma' part o' marriage, dominie. There was something in Maggie that I was aye lookin' for, but cud never find. Aye, I tried to find it in other lassies, but I never fund it."

"What was it you wanted to find, Dauvit?"

Dauvit paused.

"Ye micht call it a soul," he said. "Oh, aye," he went on, "Maggie was a bonny lassie wi' a heart o' gold, but she hadna a soul. Wud ye like to ken what stoppit me speerin' her that nicht as we cam through Zoar? Man, I said to mysel: When we come to the toll bar I'll tak Maggie in my arms and say: 'Maggie, I want ye, lassie!'"

He had to light his pipe here.

"Weelaweel, we got to the toll bar and I said: 'Maggie, we'll sit doon on the bank for a while.' So we sat doon, and I was just tryin' to screw up my courage when she pointed to the settin' sun. 'I'd like a dress like that, only bonnier,' she said. Man, dominie, I looked at that sunset wi' its gold and purple . . . and syne I kent that Maggie was nae wife for me. I kent that she had nae soul."

After a time I remarked: "And so, Dauvit, you are a bachelor because you were a poet!"

He busied himself with the paper sole.

"Maggie married Bob Wilson the farmer o' East Mains. Aye, and the marriage turned oot a happy one, for Bob never rose abune neeps and tatties in his life." Dauvit sighed. "But I sometimes used to look at the twa o' them when their bairns were roond their knees, and syne I used to gie a big *Dawm!* and ging back to my wee hoose and mak my ain tea."

"It doesna pay to hae a soul, dominie," he added with a short laugh.

"Perhaps you could have given her a soul, Dauvit," I said.

He shook his head with decision.

"Na, dominie, a soul is something ye're born wi'; if it isna there it canna be put there. You say that I'm a poet, and you may be richt; there may be a wee bit o' the artist in me, and ye never heard o' an artist that was happily married. Wumman and art are opposites, and a man canna marry both."

"That is true, Dauvit. But art is the feminine side of a man's nature; it is the woman in him . . . and the woman is superfluous to him, for she becomes the rival of the woman in himself."

This thought impressed Dauvit.

"Noo I understand Rabbie Burns," he cried. "Rabbie cudna love a wumman because he loved the wumman in himsel. She was the wife that bore his bairns—his poems." He paused, and a pained look came to his face. "There may be a poet in me, dominie," he said ruefully, "but she has borne me nae bairns. I am ane o' the mute inglorious Miltons . . . and I wud ha' been better if I had married Maggie and talked aboot neeps and tatties a' my life."

"You couldn't have done it, Dauvit," I said as I rose to go.

From the door I looked back at the old man as he stared at the fender.

* * * * *

One of the analysts says that the flirt is suffering from a mother complex. He has never got over his infantile love for his mother, and he is always trying to find the mother again in women. Hence he is like a bee, sipping at one flower and then flying on to another.

I suspect that many a bachelor is a bachelor because his early love is fixed on the mother. Few mothers realise the danger of coddling their children. I have heard grown men dying in pain call on their mothers. It is a hard task for parents, but they must always try to break their children's fixation upon them.

Women having father-complexes are common. The other day I met a girl who had no interest in young men; all her interest was in men with beards. No matter what the conversation was about she managed to mention her father. . . "Father says!" She will probably marry a man twice her age. It is well-known that boys of seventeen often fall in love with women of thirty, while adolescent girls usually fall in love with men of thirty. They are not really in love; they are looking for a substitute for the mother or father.

The psychology of the man of forty who falls in love with the girl of sixteen is more difficult to grasp. I think that in most cases the man's love interest is fixed away back in childhood; often the girl of sixteen is a substitute for a beloved sister. Perhaps on the other hand, a man of forty's paternal instinct has been starved so long that he wants to find at once a wife and a child.

Few of us realise how much of our love interest is fixed in the past. Think of the men who want to be mothered by their wives . . . they generally address their wives as "Mother." I know happily married men who are psychically children; "mother" won't allow them to carry coals or wash dishes or brush clothes; she treats them as they unconsciously desire to be treated—as babes.

It may be that Dauvit has a strong mother complex. He often talks of his mother, and more than once I have heard him say that she was the best woman he had ever known. It may be that he was unconsciously looking for the mother in Maggie and the other girls, and failed to find her. Maggie's remark about the sunset and the dress was not enough to stifle his love declaration. The soul he longed to find in Maggie may have been the soul of the mother he knew as an infant . . . the soul of his ideal woman.

The more I see of men the less importance I pay to their conscious reasons for attitudes. "I hate Brown; he never washes"; "I dislike Mrs. Smith; she uses bad language." "Murphy is a rotter; he has no manners." Statements like these are rationalisations; the real reason for the dislike lies deeper in every case.

VI.

The law courts have re-introduced flogging for criminals. To the best of my knowledge no member of the law profession has protested. If there is a reform movement within the law I never heard of it.

The curse of law is that it works according to precedent, and it is therefore conservative. Our judges hand out sentences in blissful ignorance of later psychology. Last week a boy of eleven was birched for holding up another boy of nine on the highway and demanding tuppence or his life. The attitude of the bench is that fear of another flogging will prevent that boy from turning highwayman again. I admit that fear will cure him of that special vice, but what the bench does not know is that the boy's anti-social energy will take another form. Every act of man is prompted by a wish, and very often this wish is unconscious. And all the birching in the world will not destroy a wish; the most it can do is to change its form.

Without an analysis of the boy no one can tell what unconscious wish impelled him to turn highwayman, but speaking generally a boy expresses his self-assertion in terms of anti-social behaviour only when his education has been bad. I believe that all juvenile delinquency is due to bad education. Our schools enforce passivity on the child; his creative energy is bottled up. No boy who has tools and a bench to work with will express himself by smashing windows. Delinquency is merely displaced social conduct; the motive of the little boy who turned highwayman was essentially the motive of the boy who builds a boat.

Ah! but we have Industrial Schools for bad boys!

I spent an evening with an Industrial School boy of thirteen not long ago. It was an unlovely tale he told me of his life in school. I got the impression of a building half-prison, half-barracks. No one was allowed to go out unless to football matches when the school team was playing. Punishment was stern and frequent.

"One old guy, 'e sends you to the boss for punishment and says you gave 'im an insubordinate look, and you ain't allowed to deny wot 'e says."

"Look here, Jim," I said, "suppose I took you to a free school to-morrow, a school where you could do what you liked, what's the first thing you would do?"

A wild look came into his eyes.

"I'd lay out the blarsted staff," he said tensely.

"But," I laughed, "what would be the point of laying me out if I gave you freedom? What have you got against *me*?"

"Oh," he said, "I thought you meant if I got freedom in the Industrial School!"

That school is condemned; if a school produces one boy who hates and fears its teachers, it is a bad school.

I think of the other way, the Homer Lane way.

Homer Lane was superintendent of the little Commonwealth in Dorset. He attended the juvenile courts and begged the magistrates to hand over to him the worst cases they had. He took the children down to Dorset and gave them freedom. He refused to lay down any laws, and naturally the beginning of the Commonwealth was chaos. Lane joined in the anti-social behaviour; he became one of the gang. When the citizens thought that their best way of expressing themselves was to smash windows, Lane helped them to smash them. His marvellous psychological insight will best be illustrated by the story of Jabez.

Jabez was a thoroughly bad character; he had been thief and highwayman, a bully who could fight with science. He came to the Commonwealth and was astonished. He found boys and girls working hard all day, and making their own laws at their citizen meetings at night. Jabez could not understand it, and not understanding he felt hostile.

The citizens lived in cottages, and one night Lane went over to the cottage in which Jabez lived. They were having tea, and Lane sat down beside Jabez.

"What are you always grousing about, Jabez?" he asked. "Don't you like the Commonwealth?"

"No," said Jabez viciously.

"What's wrong with it?"

"It's too respectable for me," said Jabez, and his eyes wandered to the table. "Them fancy cups and saucers! Wot's the good o' things like that to me? I'd like to smash the whole lot o' them."

Lane rose from the table, walked to the fireplace, took up the poker and handed it to Jabez.

"Smash them," he said.

Jabez had all eyes turned towards him. He seized the poker and smashed his cup and saucer.

"Excellent!" cried Lane, "Jabez is making the Commonwealth a better place," and he pushed forward another cup and saucer. These were at once smashed, and Lane proceeded to shove forward the other dishes. But by this time Jabez was beginning to feel queer. Breaking dishes was good fun when you were breaking laws, but here there was no law to break, and Jabez felt that he was doing a foolish thing. He wanted to stop, but he could not see how he was to stop with dignity. Fortunately one of the other inmates of the cottage came to his aid.

"It's all very well for you, Mr. Lane," she said, "but this isn't your cottage, and you are making Jabez break our dishes."

Jabez hailed the idea with delight; he now had an excellent excuse for stopping.

"Right you are!" cried Lane cheerfully, "Jabez will break something else," and he took out his gold watch and placed it on the table.

"Smash that, Jabez."

"No," said Jabez, "I won't smash your watch."

Now Jabez had a saying that if a man were dared to do a thing and he didn't do it he was a coward.

"I dare you to smash the watch."

Jabez seized the poker again.

"What! You dare me!"

"Yes, I dare you."

He looked at the watch for a few seconds; then he threw down the poker and rushed from the room.

Poor Jabez was killed in France. I saw the letters that he wrote to Lane from the front, and they were the letters of a decent, good boy.

The early history of Jabez was one of constant suppression. Authority was always stepping in and saying: "Don't do that!" As a result Jabez at the age of seventeen was psychically an infant. The infantile desire to break things was suppressed, but it lived on in the unconscious, and years later Jabez found himself behaving like a child of three. The cure was to encourage him to act in his infantile way; by smashing a few cups Jabez got rid of his long pent up infantile wish to destroy. Discipline would have kept the childish wish underground; freedom led to the expression of the wish.

Homer Lane is the apostle of Release. He holds that Authority is fatal for the child; suppression is bad; the only way is to allow the child freedom to express itself in the way it wants to. And because I count among my friends boys and girls who once went to the Little Commonwealth as criminals, I believe that Lane is right. I also believe that the schools will come to see that he was right . . . somewhere about the year 2500.

* * * * *

Conversation to-night in Dauvit's shop turned on Spiritualism. Dauvit is a firm believer, and he often goes to Dundee and Aberdeen to attend séances.

"It's just a lot o' blethers," said Jake Tosh contemptuously. "When ye're deid ye're deid, and that's a' aboot it. Na, na, Dauvit, them that sees ghosts is either drunk or daft."

"That's just yer ignorance, Jake," said Dauvit. "Do ye ken whaur Brazil is?"

"Wha is he?" asked Jake puzzled.

"It's no a he; it's a place. I asked ye that question just to prove that a man that doesna ken his ain world canna speak wi' ony authority o' the next world. Yer mind's ower narrow, Jake; ye've no vision."

"Na, na, Dauvit," laughed Jake, "it winna do. Spooks and things is just a curran nonsense, and no sane man wud believe in them. What do you say, dominie?"

"I am willing to believe that the dead do communicate," I said.

Jake was thoroughly amused.

"It's a queer thing," he said musingly, "that the more eddication a man has the more he believes in rubbish. Here's Dauvit here, a man that reads Shakespeare and Burns and Carlyle, and the dominie there that went through a college, and the both o' you believe things that I stoppit believin' when I was sax year auld. Then there's Sir Oliver Lodge, and Conan Doyle. Oh, aye, the Bible was quite richt when it said: Much learning hath made them mad."

"What do you think happens to the dead, Jake?" I asked.

"As the tree falleth so it lies," quoted Jake. "There's only the twa places after death; if ye're good ye go to Heaven; if ye're bad ye go to Hell. And that's why I say that thae messages from the deid are rubbish, cos if a man's in Heaven he's no going to leave a place like that to come doon to speak to a daft auld cobbler like Dauvit in a wee room doon in Dundee. And if a man's in Hell the Devil will tak good care that he doesna get oot."

I wondered to find that Dauvit had no answer to this. I guessed that Dauvit's silence was due to his early training. He was brought up in the old stern Scots way, and although he has now rejected the old beliefs intellectually, his unconscious still clings to them emotionally. I fancy that if I were very very ill I might go back to my childish fear of Hell-fire, for, in illness old emotions return, and intellect flees. Dauvit would no doubt react in the same way.

* * * * *

Many people seem to have a decided fear of psycho-analysis. A mother writes me from London saying that she would like to send her girl to my new school, only she is afraid that I shall attempt to analyse the children.

The fear of psycho-analysis comes from the general belief that Freud traces every neurosis to early sex experiences. Whether Freud is right or not does not concern the teacher; he deals with normal children, and to try to analyse a normal child appears to me to be unnecessary. The teacher's job is to see that the children are free from fear and free to create; if he does his task well he is preventing neurosis.

A neurosis is the outcome of repression; the neurotic is a person whose libido or life force is bottled up; he can be cured only by letting his pent up emotions free. The aim of education is to allow emotional release, so that there will be no bottling up, and no future neurosis; and this release comes through interest. The boy who hates algebra and has to work examples is getting no release whatever, for his mind is divided; his attention goes to his quadratic equations, but his interest is elsewhere.

Hence I do not think analysis is necessary when children are being freely educated. In an exceptional case a little analysis will do good. If I see a child unhappy, moody, anti-social, a thief, a bully, I consider it my job to make an attempt to find out what is at the back of his mind. With a young boy it is not advisable to tell him the whole truth about himself; the teacher discovers the truth by watching the child at play, by studying his wishes as expressed in his writing, by noting his attitude to his playmates. When he has made his diagnosis the teacher can then make the necessary changes in the boy's environment.

I recall the case of Tommy, aged ten. His class was constructing a Play Town after the fashion set by Caldwell Cook in his delightful book *The Play Way*. Tommy worked with enthusiasm, too much enthusiasm, for he pinched the girls' sand for his railway track. The girls objected, and a regular wordy battle took place. Tommy felt that he was beaten, and he ceased work.

I was not very much surprised when the girls came and told me that Tommy was shying bricks at the railway line he had been so keen on constructing. Tommy was brought up before the assembled class, and they voted unanimously that he be forbidden to approach within ten yards of Play Town. Tommy grinned maliciously. That night the town appeared to have been the victim of an earthquake.

I went to Tommy.

"Why don't you like the Play Town?" I asked.

"Because the girls are too bossy," he said. "It was my town; I began it, and I don't see why they should be in it at all."

"And you want a Play Town all to yourself?" I asked.

"Yes."

"Right ho," I said easily. "Why not start to build one?"

His eyes lit up, and away he ran to lay his foundations. He worked eagerly all day, but at night he seemed dissatisfied.

"I haven't got any railway or houses; Christo won't lend me a bit of his railway, and Gerda has all the houses."

I left him to work out his problem. In the morning he solved it; Christo wouldn't lend him any rails, but if Tommy liked he, Christo, would run his line up to Tommy's town from the class town. Tommy readily agreed. In a week's time Tommy's town was a suburb of the bigger town, and Tommy was appointed President of the whole state. He spent many an hour building his bridges and digging his tunnels. At first he would allow no one to enter his suburb, but in a few days he ceased to claim it as his own, and he worked as a member of the gang.

I think that most anti-social children are like Tommy: when their self-assertion is threatened they react with hostility. The cure for them is to direct their self-assertion to things instead of people. No boy will try to break up a ball game if he has a rabbit hutch to construct.

The danger is that the teacher will often step in when the boy ought to be left to his companions. The gang is the best disciplinarian.

One day a class and I were writing five-minute essays. I would call out a word or a phrase, and we would all start to write. The children loved the method; it allowed so much play for originality. For example, when I gave the word "broken" one girl wrote of her broken doll, another of a broken tramp, another of a broken heart; a boy wrote a witty essay on being stoney broke, another wrote of a broken window.

On this day Wolodia, a boy of eleven, did not want to write essays. I called out a word, and we started to write. Wolodia began to talk loudly.

"Stop it, man," I said impatiently, "you're spoiling our essay."

He grinned and went on talking.

"Oh, shut up!" cried Joy.

"Shan't!" he snapped, and he went on talking.

Diana rose with a determined air.

"We'll chuck him out," she said grimly, and the class seized him and heaved him out. Then they barricaded the door with desks. Wolodia made a big row by hammering on the door, and as a result we could not proceed with our writing.

"Let him in," I suggested.

The class protested.

"He'll sit like a lamb for the rest of the period," I said.

They took away the desk and Wolodia came in. He went to his seat . . . and not a sound came from him during the rest of the period. This incident impressed me greatly; my complaint, Joy's complaint did not affect him, but when the gang was against him he was defeated. It was a beautiful instance of the force of public opinion.

Cases of stealing should be treated by analysis. Moral lectures are useless; the cause lies in the unconscious, and the moral lecture does not touch the unconscious. Nor does punishment affect the root cause of the delinquency. The teacher must dig down into the child's unconscious in order to find the cause.

An illuminating book for all teachers and parents to read is Healy's *Mental Disorders and Misconduct*. He shows that stealing is very often a symptomatic act. The mechanism of many cases is something like this: a child has been punished for sexual activities; later he breaks into a store and steals an article. Sex activities and thieving have this in common, that they are both forbidden, but the boy has found that much more ado is made about sex activities than about stealing. So when he is actuated by a sexual urge he dare not indulge it; but his sexual wish finds a substitute; it goes out to the associated forbidden thing . . . the article on the store counter.

We see the same sort of mechanism in the neurotic patient; she fears her own sex impulses, and because she dare not admit her sex wishes into consciousness she projects her fear on to dogs or mice or rats. All phobias—fear of closed places, fear of open places, fear of heights—are displaced fears; the sufferer is really afraid of his own unconscious wishes.

I do not say that all juvenile stealing is due to repressed sex. Stealing may mean to a boy a method of self-assertion; it may mean that thus he rebels against authority of father and teacher; it may be the result of any one of a dozen causes. But whatever the cause stealing is always associated with unhappiness, and the teacher must try to cure the unhappiness.

In my *Dominie's Log* I confessed that I liked to cheat the railway company, and I excused it on the ground that "a ten-mile journey without a ticket is the only romantic experience left in a drab world." That was a delightful bit of rationalisation. The real reason for my delinquency lay in my unconscious. As a child I impotently rebelled against the authority of parents and teachers. Later in life I unconsciously identified the railway company with the authorities of my infancy. Authority said: "Don't do that or you will be smacked"; the railway company put up a notice saying: "Don't travel without a ticket or you'll be fined forty shillings."

My rebellion was really a rebellion against authority. This may seem to be a far-fetched explanation, but the fact remains that now that I have discovered the reason I have no more desire to cheat the railway company.

* * * * *

Old Jeems Broon was buried to-day, and Dauvit went to the funeral. He came back chuckling.

"What's the joke, Dauvit?" I asked.

"The burial service," laughed Dauvit. "You ken what sort o' a man Jeems was; an auld sinner if there ever was a sinner in Tarbonny, a bad auld scoondrel. Weel, Jeems hadna been at the kirk for twenty years, and of coorse the minister didna ken ony thing aboot him. So when he gave the funeral prayer he referred to auld Jeems as 'this holy man whose life stands as an example to those still tarrying in the flesh.' Goad, but I burst oot laughin'! I did that!"

"Had I been the minister," said I, "I should certainly have made a few inquiries about Jeems."

"But there's a better story than that aboot the minister," went on Dauvit with a laugh. "Mag Currie's little lassie had the diphtheria, and at the end o' the week the minister was asked to come oot to tak' a burial service in Mag's bed room. Man, he was eloquent! He spoke earnestly aboot this flower plucked before it had reached its full bloom, this innocent life so sadly cut off; he was most touchin' when he turned to Mag and her man and said: 'Mourn not for those hands that never did wrong, the lisping tongue that never spoke evil, the wide pure eyes that looked their love for you.'"

"I suppose the parents broke down at that," I said.

"Not they!" chuckled Dauvit, "for the corpse wasna their lassie ava; it was auld Drucken Findlay the lodger."

I always like to hear Dauvit talk about ministers, and I encouraged him to go on.

"It's a very queer thing, dominie, that a body ay wants to laugh at the wrong time. In the kirk and at a funeral—that's when I want to laugh.

"I mind when the minister was awa' for his holidays, and there was an auld minister frae the Heelands cam' to tak' his place. This auld man had a habit o' readin' a verse and syne stoppin' to explain it to the congregation.

"Weel aweel, wan Sunday he was readin' a chapter frae the Auld Testament, and he cam' to the words: 'And the Angel of the Lord appeared unto Hosea.' So he looks at the congregation ower his specs and he says: 'The Angel of the Lord appeared unto Hosea.' Now, prethren, we must ask ourselves this important question: Was Hosea afraid? No, Hosea was not afraid. *You* would have been afraid, prethren; I would have been afraid. You and I would have begun to quake and tremble, but Hosea was not afraid; he was a prave man, a pold man. When we are in trouble let us remember that Hosea was not afraid.'

"So the auld man he turns ower the page and reads the next verse: 'And Hosea was sore afraid.'"

"What did he say then?" I asked.

"He was a cunnin' auld deevil," said Dauvit, "for he gave a bit cough and says: 'Prethren, that is a wrong translation from the original Hebrew.'"

"I don't think you like ministers, Dauvit," I said.

He paused in his efforts to place a new needle in his sewing-machine.

"No, man, I do not," he said slowly. "Nowadays the kirk is just a job like anything else; men go in for it for the loaves and fishes mostly, and their prayers never get past the roof. And as for the congregation, the kirk is just a respectable sort o' society. I tell ye, dominie, that releegion is deid. At least, Christianity is deid. That was bound to come; flowers, folk, hooses, trees, horses, aye, and nations, have a birth, a youth, middle age, auld age, and then death. It's the law o' nature, and a religion is no exception."

"True, O philosopher!" I said, "but there is always new life, and new life comes from the old. The flower dies and its seed lives; man dies and his seed inherit the earth. Christianity dies and—and what?"

"That may be," he said thoughtfully. "It may be that the new religion will grow from the seed o' the deid Christianity; that I canna say. What I do say is that ministers are oot-o'-date; they are doin' useless labour . . . when they're no fishin' and curlin'."

VII.

Duncan came over to-night, and he asked my advice about books.

"What books would you advise a teacher to buy?" he asked.

"There are scores of good books," I replied, "but no teacher can afford to buy them."

"I know," he said crossly; "I've had a row with the Income Tax people. I asked for a rebate of ten pounds for necessary school books, and they wouldn't allow it, although I'm told that if a London merchant buys a London Directory he gets a rebate for the amount."

"I agree that it is unjust," I said, "but the new Income Tax proposals allow twenty pounds a year for teachers' books."

"Just tell us what you would advise a teacher to spend his twenty quid on," said Macdonald.

"It depends on his tastes," I said. "If his subject is History he will buy history books; if his subject is behaviour, he'll buy psychology books."

"Give us an idea of your own library," said Duncan.

I sat down and wrote out a list from memory.

It ran as follows:—

BOOKS ON EDUCATION:—

The Play Way, by Caldwell Cook.
The Path to Freedom in the School, by Norman MacMunn.
What Is and What Might Be, by Edmond Holmes.
Montessori's three volumes.
An Adventure in Education, by J. H. Simpson.

BOOKS ON PSYCHO-ANALYSIS AND PSYCHOLOGY:

Freud's *Interpretation of Dreams, Psychopathology of Everyday Life, Three Contributions to the Sexual Theory*.
Jung's *Psychology of the Unconscious, Studies in Word Association, Analytical Psychology*.
Frink's *Morbid Fears and Compulsions*.
Maurice Nicoll's *Dream Psychology*.
Morton Prince's *The Unconscious*.
Pfister's *The Psycho-analytic Method*.
Ernest Jones' *Psycho-analysis*.
Ferenczi's *Contributions to Psycho-analysis*.

Wilfred Lay's *The Child's Unconscious Mind.*
Moll's *The Sexual Life of the Child.*
Adler's *The Neurotic Constitution.*
Bernard Hart's *The Psychology of Insanity.*

CROWD PSYCHOLOGY:—
The Crowd in Peace and War, Martin Conway.
Instincts of the Herd in Peace and War, Trotter.
The Crowd, Gustave le Bon.

GENERAL PSYCHOLOGY:—
Psychology and Everyday Life, Swift.
Textbook of Psychology, James.
The Boy and His Gang, Puffer.
Mental Conflicts and Misconduct, Healy.
The Individual Delinquent, Healy.
Rational Sex Ethics, Robie.
Social Psychology, McDougall.
The Play of Man, Groos.

"That's too much for me," said Duncan. "I couldn't afford a quarter of these books. What books would you recommend if you had to choose half a dozen for a hard-up dominie?"

I thought for a little, and then I replied: "Bernard Hart's *The Psychology of Insanity,* two bob; Frink's *Morbid Fears and Compulsions,* a first-rate book on analysis, a guinea; *The Crowd in Peace and War,* by Sir Martin Conway, eight and six; Healy's *Mental Conflicts and Misconduct,* ten and six; and Wilfred Lay's *The Child's Unconscious Mind,* ten and six."

"But," cried Duncan, "I don't want to set up an asylum! What's the good of books on insanity and morbid fears to a teacher?"

I explained that the titles of Hart's and Frink's books were misleading, although the difference between the mind of the lunatic and the mind of the average man is merely one of degree. Bernard Hart shows that the lunatic has the same faults as we have, only more so. Frink's book is badly named; it is an excellent work on mind mechanisms. Any teacher who reads these six books with understanding will never again use a strap on a pupil. If I were Education Minister, I should present every school in Britain with a copy of each of the six.

Macdonald asked if I had any books on hypnotism and suggestion.

"No," I said, "but I have read them through a library. I don't believe in either because they do not touch root causes. We are all suffering from bottled up infantile emotion, and analysis goes to the root of the matter; it makes what is unconscious conscious, and enables the patient to re-educate himself, to use the old repressed emotion up in his daily life. Analysis means release. Suggestion does not touch the root repressed emotion, and I fancy that after suggestion the symptom merely changes. A man has a phobia of cats. By suggestion I can dispel his fear of cats, but the fear is transferred to something else, and he then has an exaggerated fear of catching tuberculosis. Unless the ancient cause becomes conscious it is not released.

"We see suggestion working in our schools daily. By suggestion parents and teachers force the child to inhibit his gross sexual wishes, and in a short time the child accepts the ideals of his masters. At first he inhibits a desire because father thinks it naughty; later he inhibits it because he himself thinks it naughty. But the gross sexual wish lives on in the unconscious . . . hence the neurosis, hence the respectable old men who are imprisoned for showing gross pictures to children, hence the frequent indecent assaults on children. All these unfortunate people are suffering from the results of early suggestion—the suggestion that sex is sin. That primitive sex impulses can be sublimated I admit, but the teacher's job is not to preach that sex activities are evil; his job is to help the child to use up his primitive sex energy in creative work."

* * * * *

What is education's chief aim? The reply generally given is that education's aim is to help a child to live its life fully. Yet it seems to me that that reply does not go far enough; I think that the aim should be to help a child to live its cosmic life fully, to live for others. Every human is egocentric, selfish. No human ever rises above selfishness, only there are degrees of selfishness. I buy a motor-cycle because I am selfish; and you found a hospital for orphans because you are selfish. It is my pleasure to have a Sunbeam; it is yours to help the poor. Your selfishness has become altruism; that is, in pleasing yourself you have managed to please others. The aim in education is not to abolish selfishness; it is to educe the selfishness that is altruistic. Hence it may be said that education's chief aim is to teach one how to love. No, that won't do; no one can teach another how to love; the teacher's job is to evoke love. This he can do only by loving. If I hate my pupils I evoke hate from them; if I love them I evoke love from them in return.

Is it possible to love your neighbour as yourself? It is when you know yourself. You hate in others what you hate in yourself, and you love in others what is lovable in yourself. So that in loving your neighbour you are loving yourself.

If, then, the teacher's first aim is to evoke the love of his pupils, he must know himself, and knowing must love himself. Every day pupils are suffering because of the teacher's hatred of himself.

Dominie Brown rises in the morning surly and unhappy. He complains about the bacon and eggs at breakfast . . . no, the red herring; dominies cannot afford bacon and eggs . . . and Mrs. Brown makes unpleasant remarks. Brown crosses the road to school with thunder on his face, and the children shiver in terror all morning.

If Brown could sit down calmly to think out his bad mood, he would realise that he was punishing the children because he was worsted in his word battle with his wife. And *he would be quite wrong*. The truth would be that he was punishing the children because he was at war with himself. His early morning ugly mood betrayed a mental conflict. Hating himself, he hated his wife; his hate evoked her hate . . . and thus the circle was completed.

We might trace all the futilities, all the stupidities of mankind, all the wars and crimes and injustices to man's ignorance of self. To know all is to forgive all. Christ condemned no one because he was at peace with himself. Yet, I suddenly remember that He whipped the money-changers out of the Temple. This incident is comforting, for it shows that the most lovable man who ever lived betrayed one human frailty on one occasion at least. But now I am preaching again.

* * * * *

I went to see Charlie Chaplin in "Shoulder Arms" last night. Charlie is an artist of high quality; for once I think as the crowd thinks. But I leave the crowd when it comes to appreciating the "moving human dramas" in five parts.

The cinema must be reckoned with in any educational scheme. One may learn more about crowd psychology from attendance at cinemas than from reading books on crowd psychology. The cinema is popular because it encourages day-dreaming or phantasy. There are two kinds of thinking, reality thinking and phantasy or day-dreaming. Phantasying is the easier of the two; I can sit for hours building castles in Spain, and I never grow tired; but if I have to sit down and think out the Theory of Quadratics I soon become weary. In reality thinking the intellect is active, but in day-dreaming emotion is in control. Day-dreaming gets nowhere; the asylums are full of day-dreamers who spend their hours constructing beautiful phantasies. In childhood phantasy is supreme. Bobby turns the nursery into a jungle; the sofa is a tiger, the chairs are lions, the rocking-horse is an elephant. It is all real to him. And in later years Bobby often returns to his childish phantasying. We all do. What young lover has not phantasied a burning mansion where his lady love is imprisoned? Have we not all clambered up the water pipes and rescued her from the flames?

The world of the theatre is a phantasy world. With the rising of the curtain we forget our outside life; we live the part of the hero or the heroine. To this day I always leave a theatre with a vague depression of spirits; everyday humdrum life chills me when I come out to the street. Reality is always difficult to face. The great popularity of the cinema is due to this human desire for make-believe. Cinema-going is a regression to the infantile; we return to the childish phase where the wish was all powerful. In the cinema the villain is always worsted; the wronged heroine always falls into the hero's arms at the end. Life for most of us means trials and sorrows and conflicts, and we long to return to the nursery phase where life was what we wished it to be. The cinema and the public-house are the most convenient doors by which we can regress.

The "moving drama" is the other side of the industrial picture. Life for the masses means dirt and disease, ugly factories, sordid homes, mean streets. The moving drama takes the masses away from grim reality; they see beautifully gowned women in drawing-rooms; they see the King reviewing his regiments; they see wild and free cowboys chasing Red Indians. For two hours they live . . . and then they go out again into their world of mere existence. And it is all wrong, tragically wrong. The cinema craze means that life is too ugly to face; it means that the masses are fleeing from reality and to flee from reality is fatal. Day-dreams are laudable only when they come true. If the masses day-dreamed of an economic Utopia and forthwith set about building a New Jerusalem, their phantasies would become realities; but the moving human drama never leads to building; it is raw whisky swallowed to bring oblivion. The moving human drama will live and flourish so long as mankind tolerates the slavery of industrialism. It is a powerful weapon for capitalism; like the church and the public-house, it keeps the wage-slaves quiet.

* * * * *

To-night the conversation in Dauvit's shop turned to the subject of honours.

"They tell me," said Jake Tosh, "that you can buy a knighthood, or a peerage for that matter."

"Yea, man!" said Willie Simpson, the joiner and undertaker from Tillymains.

"So there's no muckle chance o' you getting ane, Willie," said Dauvit.

The joiner smoked thoughtfully for a while.

"Na, Dauvit," he said, "there's little chance o' an undertaker gettin' a title. You would think na that the man that coffined the likes o' Lloyd George wud get a knighthood."

Dauvit cackled.

"Honours are sold, as Jake says; they are never given for public services."

I am afraid the joke was lost on most of the assembly. Jake failed to see it. It is said that Jake has been known to laugh at a joke only once, and that was when the earth gave way beneath the minister's feet when he was conducting a service at a grave-side, and he fell into the open grave.

"Undertakin'," continued the joiner, "is a verra queer trade."

Jake shivered.

"I dinna ken how ye can do it," he said; "man, it wud gie me the scunners."

"Man, ye soon get accustomed to it," said the joiner. "Of course, it has its limitations; ye canna verra weel advertise in the front page o' *The Daily Mail*, but, man, it's what ye micht call a safe trade."

"How safe?" I asked.

"Oh, ye never need to worry aboot yer custom; it's aye there. Noo in other lines the laws o' supply and demand are tricky. I mind a gey puckle years syne there was a craze for walkin'-sticks wi' ebony handles. Weel, I went doon to Dundee and bocht ten pund worth o' ebony, and afore the wood was delivered the fashion had changed, and the men were all buyin' cheese-cutter bonnets, so here was I left wi' ten pund worth o' ebony on my hands . . . and if I hadna sold it to Davie Lamb the cabinet-maker for thirteen pund I micht ha' lost the money. Noo, in my trade there's no sudden change o' fashion as ye micht say; the demand is what ye micht call constant, and that's what makes me say it is a safe trade."

Dauvit winked to me surreptitiously.

"Noo, joiner," he said, "will ye tell me wan thing? I want to ken the inner workin's o' an undertakker's mind. When somebody is verra ill, what's your attitude? I mean to say, do ye sort o' look on the illness wi' hope or what? When ye see a fine set-up man on the road, do ye look at him wi' a professional eye and say to yersell: 'Sax feet by twa; a bonny corp!'?"

"I'm no so bad as that, Dauvit," he laughed, "though I dinna mind sayin' that I've sometimes been a wee bit disappointed when somebody got better. On the other hand, when big Tamson was badly, I keepit prayin' that he wud get better."

"An unbusinesslike thing to do," I laughed.

"Aweel," said the joiner, "big Tamson weighed aboot saxteen stone, and at the time I hadna the wood."

"I dinna like to hear aboot things like that," said Jake Tosh nervously; "things like that give me the creeps, and besides it's no a proper way to speak."

Dauvit turned to me.

"Man, dominie, it's a queer thing, but the more religious a man is the less he likes to hear aboot death. Jake here is an elder o' the auld kirk; he's on the straight and narrow path; he's going straight to heaven when he dees . . . and I never saw onybody so feared o' death as Jake is. How wud ye explain that?"

"I think," I replied, "that it is due to the fact that Jake has been brought up in the fear of the Lord."

"Exactly," nodded Dauvit. "It's my belief that most religious fowk are religious not becos they want specially to play harps in the next world, but becos they dinna want to be roasted."

Dauvit's philosophy comes pretty near that of Edmond Holmes. In *What Is and What Might Be* Holmes argues that our education system is founded on the Old Testament. Man is a sinner, prone to evil; a stern angry God chastises him when he transgresses. Education treats children as sinners; it punishes the wrongdoer. I believe Holmes is right, only he does not trace back education far enough. The God of the Old Testament was a man-made God (Jung says that man makes his God in his own image; his God is his ego-ideal).

The genesis of education is not the God of the Old Testament; it is the unconscious wish of the primitive men who invented that God. The religion of the Old Testament is a father complex religion; God is the hated and feared father, the authority who punishes, the provider of food and clothing, the maker of laws. Authority always makes the governed inferior and dependent; the man with a father complex cannot stand alone; he must always flee to his father or father substitute when he meets a difficulty. Thus does the Christian act; he seeks the Father; he places his burden on the Lord; he avoids responsibility. The Hebraic religion and our modern education both demand that the individual shall avoid responsibility; the good Christian and the good schoolboy must obey the Law. I think that if the world is to be free the church and the school must aim at breaking the power of the Father.

* * * * *

"Look here, Mac," I said last night, "I am going to pay you for my board."

Mac protested vigorously.

"You'll do nothing of the kind," he said firmly.

I went to the kitchen and made the offer to his wife, and she also protested.

This morning I cycled to Dundee and bought a knife-cleaner and a vacuum cleaner. They arrived to-night, and Mrs. Mac gave a gasp of delight. Mac tried to frown, but he could not manage it. Both protested against what they called my idiotic kindness, but their protests were half-hearted.

It is a strange thing that money itself is considered a sordid thing. Why should Mac refuse five pounds with anger, and accept a ten pound gift with pleasure? If anyone wants to study the psychological meaning of money I recommend Chapter XL. in Dr. Ernest Jones' *Psycho-analysis*. In the unconscious, at any rate, money is assuredly "filthy lucre."

* * * * *

A teacher should know very little about the subject he professes to teach. In my London school I succeeded a line of excellent teachers of drawing. I had not been long in the school when Di, aged 15, looked over my shoulder one day and said: "Rotten! You can't draw for nuts!"

A week later Malcolm looked at a water colour of mine.

"You've got a horrible sense of colour," he said brightly.

Then I began to wonder why everyone in school was much more keen on drawing and painting than they had ever been in the days of the skilled teachers. The conclusion I came to was that my bad drawing encouraged the children. I remembered the beautiful copy-book headlines of my boyhood, and I recalled the hopelessness of ever reaching the standard set by the lithographers. No child should have perfection put before him. The teacher should never try to teach; he should work alongside the children; he should be a co-worker, not a model.

Most teachers set themselves on a pedestal. They think that they lose dignity if they are not able to answer every question that a child puts to them. One result is that the child develops a dangerous inferiority complex. I knew one boy who was a duffer at mathematics. His weakness was due to the inferiority he felt when he saw the learned mathematical master juggle with figures as easily as a conjurer juggles with billiard balls. The little chap lost all hope, and when he worked problems he worked solely to escape punishment.

The difficulty is that if a teacher works at a subject year after year he is bound to become an expert. The only remedy I can think of is to make each teacher take up a new subject at the beginning of every school year. By the time that he had been master of Mathematics, History, Drawing, English, French, German, Latin, Geography, Chemistry, Physics, Psychology, Physiology, Eurhythmics, Music, Woodwork, it would be time to retire . . . with a pension or a psychosis. The late

Sir William Osier said that a man was too old at forty; my experience leads me to conclude that many a teacher is too old at twenty.

I sometimes think that every man has a certain definite psychic age fixed for him by the Almighty before he is born. I know a man of seventy who is psychically five years old, and he will never grow older. I know a boy of ten who is psychically sixty years old, and he will never grow younger.

Psycho-analysis is doing a lot of good, but I fear that it may do a lot of harm, for, one fine day Professor Freud or Dr. Jung will get hold of Peter Pan, take him by the back of the neck, and say: "My lad, you've got a fixation somewhere; you are the super-regression-to-the-infantile specimen; you've got to be analysed." And then Peter will grow up and read *The Daily News* and own an allotment and a season ticket.

When we know all about psychology, the world will be rather dull. The Freudians have said that the play of *Hamlet* is the result of Shakespeare's Œdipus Complex. If Shakespeare had not had an unconscious hatred of his father, *Hamlet* would never have been written. In other words, if Bacon had discovered the psychology of the unconscious, Shakespeare might have been analysed and forthwith might have gone in for keeping bees instead of writing plays.

It is the neurotic who leads the world; he is a rebel and he is an idealist. Yet when you analyse him you find what a poor devil he is. His noble crusade against vivisection is due to the abnormal strain of cruelty he is repressing in himself; his passion for Socialism comes from his infant fear of and rebellion against his father. The ardent suffragette who smashes windows in a just cause is merely doing so because the vote is a symbol of freedom from an arrogant husband.

What I want to know is this: In the year 5000, when everyone is free from repressions and suppressions, will there be any rebels to spur humanity on? But then if humanity is free from unconscious urges there will be no need for rebels, for there will be no crime or prison or wars or politicians. Every man will be a superman.

I firmly believe that Freud's discovery will have a greater influence on the evolution of humanity than any discovery of the last ten centuries. Freud has begun the road that leads to superman, and, although Jung and Adler and others have begun to lead sideroads off the main track, the sideroads are all leading forward. Theirs is a great message of hope.

And yet, nineteen hundred years ago Jesus Christ gave the world a New Psychology . . . and none of us have tried to apply it to our souls.

VIII.

Mac came across a vulgar word in a composition he was correcting to-night, and it seemed to alarm him. He could not understand why I laughed, and I explained to him that I liked vulgarity.

I remember when a high-minded mother came into my class-room in Hampstead. The highest class was writing essays. On her asking what the subject was, I replied that each pupil had a different subject. She walked round and looked over their shoulders. I saw the lady's eyebrows go up as she read titles such as these:—"I Grow Forty Feet high in One Night"; "I Edit the Greenland *Morning Frost*" (the news this boy gave was delightful); "I Interview Noah for the *Daily Mail*" (photos on back page). She nodded approvingly when she read the titles of the more serious essays. Then I saw her adjust her spectacles in great haste; she was looking over Muriel's shoulder.

"Mr. Neill," she gasped, "do you think this a suitable subject for a girl?"

I glanced at the title; it was; "Autobiography of My Nose."

"Er—what's wrong with it?" I said falteringly.

"It lends itself too readily to vulgarity," she said.

I picked up the book, and together we read the opening words.

"When first I began to run . . . ."

The high-minded lady left the room hurriedly.

I loved that class. Often I wish that I had kept their essays. One day we had a five minute essay on the subject: Waiting for My Cue. Lawrence wrote of standing on the steps in a cold sweat of fear. He had only five words to say—"The carriage waits, my lord," but he had never acted before. His cue was: "Ho! Who comes here?"

"At last," he wrote, "I heard the fateful words: 'Ho! Who comes here?' I could not move; I stood trembling on the stairs.

"'Get on, you idiot!' whispered the stage manager savagely, but still I could not move.

"'Ho! Who comes here?' repeated the fool on the stage. Still I could not move a step.

"'Ho! Who comes here?'

"Suddenly I became aware of a disturbance in the auditorium. The noise increased, and then I heard the agonising words: 'Fire! Fire!' Panic followed, and cries of terror rang out.

"But I . . . I jumped on the stage and cried: 'Hurrah! Hoo-blinking-rah!' It was the happiest moment of my life."

Sydney took a different line. Her cue was the sound of a stage kiss. Boldly she walked on, and the stage lovers glared at her, for she arrived before the kiss was finished or rather properly begun. The audience chuckled. At the next performance she determined to be less punctual. She heard the smack of the kiss, but she did not move. As she waited she heard the audience roaring with laughter, and then she realised that the poor lovers had been standing kissing each other for a full five minutes.

I must write to these dear old children to ask if they kept their essays.

* * * * *

Duncan was in to-night, and he told a school story that was new to me.

In a certain council school it was the custom for teachers to write down on the blackboard any instructions they might have for the janitor before they left at night. One night he came in and read the words: Find the L.C.M.

"Good gracious!" he growled, "has that darn thing gone and got lost again?"

That version was new to me. My own version ran thus:—

Little Willie is doing his home lessons, and he asks his father to help him with a sum. The father takes the slate in his hand and reads the words: Find the G.C.M.

"Good heavens!" he cries, "haven't they found that blamed thing yet? They were hunting for it when I was at school."

I think both versions are very good.

* * * * *

I have a strong Montessori complex. I find myself being critical of her system, and I have often wondered why. I used to think that my dislike of Montessori was a projection: I disliked a lady who raved about Montessori, and I fancied that I had transferred my dislike of the lady to poor Montessori. But now I refuse to accept that explanation; it is not good enough for me; there must be something deeper. I shall try to discover that something deeper.

When I first read Montessori's books I said to myself: "She is devoid of humour." This to me suggests a limitation in art, and I feel that Montessori is always a scientist but never an artist. Her system is highly intellectual, but sadly lacking in emotionalism. This is seen in her attitude to phantasy. She would probably argue that phantasy is bad for a child, but it is a fact that much of a child's life is lived in phantasy. Phantasy is a means of gratifying an unfulfilled wish. The kitchen-maid in her day-dream marries a prince, and, as Maurice Nicoll says in his *Dream Psychology*, to destroy her phantasy without putting something in its place is dangerous.

To a child, as to Cinderella, phantasy is a means of overcoming reality. Father bullies Willie and the boy retires into a day-dream world where he becomes an all-powerful person . . . hence the fairy tales of giants (fathers) killed by little Jacks. In later life Willie takes to drink or identifies himself with the hero of a cinema drama.

The extreme form of phantasy is insanity, where the patient completely goes over to the unreal world and becomes the Queen of the World. And it might be objected that phantasying is the first stage of insanity. Yes, but it is the last stage of poetry. Coleridge's *Kubla Khan*, one of the most glorious poems in the language, is pure phantasy. I rather fear that one day a grown-up Montessori child will prove conclusively that the feet of Maud did not, when they touched the meadows, leave the daisies rosy.

No, the Montessori world is too scientific for me; it is too orderly, too didactic. The name "didactic apparatus" frightens me.

I quote a sentence from *The New Children*, by Mrs. Radice.

"'Per carita! Get up at once!' she (Montessori) has exclaimed before now to a conscientious teacher found dishevelled on the ground with a class of little Bolshevists sitting on top of her."

In heaven's name, I ask, why get up? Life is more than meat, and education is more than matching colours and fitting cylinders into holes.

Montessori was thinking of the conscious mind of the child when she evolved her system, and the apparatus does not satisfy the whole of the child's unconscious mind. Noise is suppressed in a Montessori school, but every child should be allowed to make a noise, for noise means power to him, and he will use it only as long as it means power to him. I have watched Norman MacMunn's war orphans at Tiptree Hall at work. MacMunn, the author of *A Path to Freedom in the School*, did not say "Hush!"; his boys filled the room with noisy talk as they worked, and never have I seen children do more work with so much joy.

The Montessori teacher, when she finds that Jimmy is interfering with the work of Alice, segregates the bad Jimmy, and treats him as a sick person. But the right thing to do is to solve Jimmy's problem as well as Alice's. What is behind Jimmy's aggressiveness? Jimmy does not know, nor does the Montessori teacher, because she has been trained in the psychology of the conscious only.

Another reason why I am not wholly on the side of Montessori is, I fancy, that her religious attitude repels me. She is a church woman; she has a definite idea of right and wrong. Thus, although she allows children freedom to choose their own occupations, she allows them no freedom to challenge adult morality. But for a child to accept a ready-made code of morals is dangerous; education in morality is a thousand times more important than intellectual education with a didactic apparatus.

* * * * *

To-night Duncan came in, and as usual we talked education. I took up the subject of punishment, and condemned it on the ground that it treats effect instead of cause. After a little persuasion Duncan seemed inclined to agree with me.

"I see what you mean," he said, "but what I say is that if you abolish punishment you must also abolish reward."

"Why not?" I said. "The case against rewards is just as simple. A child should do a lesson for the joy of doing it. Milton certainly did not write *Paradise Lost* for the five pounds he got for it."

"Yes, I see that," said Duncan thoughtfully, "but what about competition? The prize at the end introduces a breezy struggle for place."

I shook my head.

"No competition! I won't have it. It makes the chap at the top of the class a prig, and gives the poor chap at the bottom an inferiority complex. No, we want to encourage not competition but co-operation. Competition leads naturally to another world war, as competition between British and American capital is doing now."

Then Duncan floored me.

"And would you discourage football because it introduces the idea of competition?" he asked.

"Of course not," I replied

"Then why discourage it in arithmetic?" he asked.

It was an arresting question, and I had to grope for an answer that would convince not only Duncan but myself. That every healthy boy likes to try his strength against his fellows is a fact that we cannot ignore. Mr. Arthur Balfour's desire to beat his golfing partner and Jock Broon's desire to spit farther than Jake Tosh are fundamentally the same desire, the desire for self-assertion. And I see that the man who comes in last in the quarter-mile race is in the same position of inferiority as the boy who is always at the bottom of the class. Yet I condemn competition in school-work while I appreciate competition in games. Why?

I think I should leave it to the children. Obviously they like to compete in games and races, but they have no natural desire to compete in lessons. It appears that some things naturally lend themselves to competition—racing, boxing, billiards, jumping, football and so on. Other things do not encourage competition. Bernard Shaw and G. K. Chesterton do not compete in the output of books; Freud and Jung do not struggle to publish the record number of analysis cases; George Robey and Little Tich do not appear together on the stage of the Palladium and try to prove which is the funnier. Rivalry there always is, but it remains only rivalry until *The Daily Mail* offers a prize for the biggest cabbage or sweet-pea, and then competition seizes suburbia.

I should therefore leave the children to discover for themselves what interests lend themselves to competition, and what interests do not. I know beforehand that of their own accord they will not introduce it into school subjects. This is in accord with my views on the authority question. I insist that the teacher will impose nothing; that his task is to watch the children find their own solution.

* * * * *

I must write down a wise saying that came from Dauvit. A rambling and ill-informed discussion of Bolshevism arose in his shop to-night. Dauvit took no part in it, but when we rose to go he said: "Tak' my word for it, Bolshevism is wrong."

"How do you make that out, Dauvit?" I asked.

"Because it's a success," he said shortly.

* * * * *

To-night the Rev. Mr. Smith, the U.F. minister, came in. He is one of the unco' guid, and to him all pleasures are sinful. It happened that I was telling Macdonald the Freudian theory of dreams when he entered, and when Mac told him what the conversation had been about, he begged me to continue. It was evident that he had never heard of dream interpretation, and he was surprised.

"And every dream has a meaning?" he asked.

"Yes," I said.

"I had a dream last night," he began, but I held up a warning hand.

"You shouldn't tell your dreams in public," I said hastily; "they may give things away that you don't want others to know."

He laughed.

"I don't mind that," he said, "I'll take the risk. Last night I dreamt that I was in a public-house among a lot of men who were telling most obscene stories. According to Freud every dream is the fulfilment of a wish. Do you mean to tell me that I wish to be in such a company?"

I explained that the dream as told is not the dream in reality, the meaning lies behind the symbolism, and it can be got at by the method of free association. I also explained that I did not believe the Freud theory, that the dream is always a wish, and suggested that Jung was a surer guide.

"According to Jung," I said, "the dream is often compensatory. In your own case you are consciously living the higher life, but there is another side of life that you are ignoring, and that is the vulgar pub side. Your dream is a hint that the vulgar side of life cannot be ignored. You may ignore it consciously, but your unconscious will seek the other side in your dreams."

This seemed to make him think.

"But the saints and martyrs!" he cried. "Think of the thousands who crucified the flesh so that they might win the everlasting crown! Do you tell me that they were all wrong?"

I lit my pipe.

"I think they were," I said, "for they merely repressed their animal life. They thought that they had conquered it, but they only buried it. The real saint is the man who faces his flesh boldly and loves it too, just as much as he loves his God."

Then the minister fled.

The interpretation of dreams is one of the most fascinating studies in the world. The method as evolved by Freud is simple, although the interpretation is anything but simple. Obviously the average dream has no meaning. You dream that a horse speaks to you, and then it turns into your brother. It is all nonsense, yet behind the nonsense is a serious meaning. Not long ago I was analysing a girl of sixteen. About a week after the analysis began she brought a dream which began thus: "I am invisible, and I have a tail that I can take off or put on."

Following the method of free association I said to her: "What comes into your mind about being invisible?"

"Oh, I've often wanted to be invisible, for then I could do what I liked; then I would be free."

Being invisible therefore meant being free.

Then I asked her associations to the tail part.

"Tail . . . monkeys at the Zoo; they are poor things always kept behind bars. Just like me. I forgot to say that my tail wasn't on in the dream."

Tail therefore meant something associated with confinement and restriction. It is significant that her tail was unattached. I took it to mean a wish-fulfilment dream; in it she got free from her neurosis.

The following night she dreamt that she was being driven in a motor car by a swanky chauffeur. They came to the bottom of a hill, and the car stopped, and she got out and walked. Her first association was: "The chauffeur had a big green coat on, one just like the coat you wear."

"So I was the chauffeur?" I asked.

She brightened at once.

"I see it!" she cried. "The car is the analysis; you are driving me away from my old life!"

"Excellent!" I said, "but don't forget that the car stopped at the bottom of the hill. What does the word hill give you?"

"Something difficult to climb. I hated climbing it and thought it a shame that the motor didn't take me up."

"Well?"

"I've got to climb to get better, haven't I?"

"That's right," I said. "I told you the other night that no analyst should give advice, and I refused when you asked me for it. In your unconscious you realise that the chauffeur is not going to take you up the hill; in other words you've got to do most of the work."

Freud holds that there is a censor standing between the conscious and the unconscious. Primitive wishes seek to come from the unconscious, but the censor holds up his hand. "No," he says, "that's too disgusting; the conscious mind couldn't stand that; it would be shocked. You must disguise yourself in harmless form!" And so the infantile sex wish is changed into a harmless dog or cycle. But if this is the case why should my little girl dream of me as a chauffeur? There was nothing disgusting about me, nothing that her conscious mind could not face.

I prefer Jung's theory. He says that we dream in symbols because symbolism is the oldest language in the world, and, as the unconscious is primitive it uses this language. We all dream of shocking things, and if the endopsychic censor were really on duty he would never allow these disgusting dreams to get through.

If I dream that my father is dead the Freudians declare that I either wish or, in the past, have wished unconsciously for my father's death. But surely so alarming a wish would be changed into a harmless form if there were a censor. One night I dreamt that an acquaintance, Murray, was dead. The first association to Murray was: "He's a lazy sort of chap." I think that all he stood for was laziness, and he was merely my own laziness symbolised. The dream was a hint to me to be up and doing, for I had been neglecting a task that I should have undertaken.

There is what might be called the cheese-and-tripe supper theory of the dream held by many people.

"There's nothing in dreams," they say, "nothing but the disorders following late supper."

A cheese-and-tripe supper will cause queer dreams, but the advocates of this theory cannot explain why a tripe supper should make me dream of—say—a tiger. Why not a lion or a mouse?

It is an accepted fact now in psychology that the dream is the working of the unconscious. Some theosophists claim that during sleep your spirit leaves your body and seeks the astral plane, but I have never seen anything resembling evidence of this. It may be a fact for all that.

Concerning the prophetic aspect of dreams I know nothing. I have heard that the night before the Tay Bridge disaster a woman dreamt that it was to take place, and she persuaded her husband not to travel by that ill-fated train, but I cannot vouch for the story. I believe, however, that the dream is prophetic in that the unconscious during the night is working out the problems of the next day. The popular saying about sleeping over a problem shows that there is a real belief in this aspect. I know a lady who was undergoing analysis. She was suffering from a father complex, that is, her infantile fixation on the father had remained with her, and unconsciously she was approving or disapproving of every man she met according as he did or did not in some way resemble her father.

For a few weeks after the analysis began she was always dreaming that she was back in her childhood home, and in her dreams she was always trying to get away from home and her father was always restraining her from going. Often the figure in the dream was not the father, but the associations always showed that the figure was standing for the father. One night the figure was the King, and her first association was: "The King's name is George. . . . That's father's name too."

This seems to be a case where the unconscious is striving to find a solution.

The way the unconscious does things is wonderful. I remember one night listening to a lecture by Homer Lane. He brought forward a new theory about education, and it was so deep that I did not quite grasp its meaning. At the time Alan, Homer Lane's youngest child, was one of the pupils in the school in which I taught. That night I dreamt that I was standing before a class. Alan was sitting in the front seat, and behind him was a boy whom in the dream I called "Homer Lane's youngest child." The new theory had become in the language of symbolism Alan's younger brother . . . in short, Lane's latest. Here again I cannot see why any censor should change a theory into a child.

* * * * *

In my *Log* I make a very, very poor statement about sex instruction. I say that children should be encouraged to believe in the stork theory of birth until the age of nine. That was a wrong belief, but then at that time I had not read Freud or Bloch or Moll. I see now that the child should be told the truth about sex whenever he asks for information. But I fear, that many modern mothers think that they have sexually educated their child when they tell him where babies come from. The physiological side of sex is the less important; you can take a child through all the usual stages—pollination of plants, fertilisation of eggs, right up to human birth, but the child will find no help in these informations when he faces his sex instinct at adolescence. Sex instruction should be psychological; it should deal with the sex instinct as one form of life force or libido. The child should be led to face it openly. It should be entirely dissociated from sin, and moral lectures should not be given.

Who is to give the instruction? That is the difficulty. Most parents and teachers cannot do it because their own sex instinct is all wrong. Make a remark about sex in the company of adults, and it will be reacted to in two ways; some will grin and laugh; others will be shocked. I hasten to add that the shocked ones are worse than the laughers. The laugh is a release of sex repressions; the shocked appearance is a compensation for an unconscious over-interest in sex. Anyway neither type is capable of talking about sex to children, and since humanity is roughly divided into prudes and sinners (not saints and sinners), there is little hope of a frank sex education for kiddies.

Many people say: "Oh, leave it to the doctors," but personally I haven't enough faith in doctors. Their attitude to sex is usually no better than the attitude of the layman. I know doctors who could give excellent instruction to children on the physiology of sex, but the only doctors of my acquaintance who could teach the psychological side are psycho-analysts or psycho-therapists of some sort.

Teachers can tackle the sex problem negatively. Sex activity is a form of life force or interest, and if a child is not finding life interesting enough there is a danger that he will regress to what is called auto-eroticism. When we remember that the sexual instinct is the creative instinct, and that creation in dancing or music or poetry or art of any kind is sublimated sex, that is sex raised to a higher power, we can readily see that one of the most important parts of a teacher's job is to provide ways and means for creation. I realise that this is not enough, but, as I say, I cannot see the way to a good sex education, until every teacher and parent has discovered his or her own sex complexes. Co-education helps, for then the commingling of the sexes affords a harmless and unconscious outlet for sex interest. But co-education is no panacea, for the sex problems of the individual child in a co-educational school are almost as immediate as those of the child from the segregated school.

IX.

This morning I was setting off for Dundee when Willie Marshall entered the compartment. He was dressed in his Sunday best, and I wondered why he was going to Dundee on a Wednesday.

"Hullo, Willie!" I cried, "what's on to-day?"

He looked troubled and angry.

"I've been summoned to serve on the jury that's tryin' that dawmed rat that stailt ten pund frae the minister," he said viciously, "and I had little need to lose a day, for I hae far mair work than I can dae. Mossbank's twa cairts cam in yestreen, and he's swearin' like onything that he maun hae them by the nicht." Willie is a joiner, and most of his work is building and repairing carts.

"So you think that Nosie Broon is guilty?" I said with a smile.

"Of coorse he is," he cried with emphasis.

"But," I said seriously, "you'll maybe alter your mind when you hear the evidence."

He grunted.

"Dawn nae fear! I'll show him that he's no to drag me awa frae ma work for nothing!"

He opened his *Dundee Courier*, and I sat and thought of the trial by jury method. I would not condemn it on the strength of Willie's dangerous misunderstanding of what it means, but I do condemn it on other grounds. Weighing evidence is a difficult enough business even for the specialist, for it is almost impossible to eliminate emotion in forming a judgment. With a jury of citizens, some of them possibly illiterate, too much depends on the advocates, or on outside causes.

During the war there was a glaring instance of this. A soldier shot the man who had been trying to steal his wife's love . . . and the verdict of the jury was Not Guilty. The emotional factor in this case was that the dead man was a German. I am not arguing that the prisoner should have been hanged or imprisoned, for I think both procedures are bad; I merely point out that in the eyes of legalism the soldier was guilty, yet the jury threw legalism overboard.

Another instance of the emotional factor over-ruling legalism is seen in the trial of the man who shot Jaures. He was acquitted. . . . Not Guilty . . . the man who slew one of the best men in Europe. On the other hand the youth who attempted to assassinate Clemenceau was sentenced to death, pardoned, and sent to penal servitude. In France therefore it is a crime to kill a politician of the right, but a virtue to kill one of the Socialist left.

Abstract justice is a figment. No jury and no judge can be impartial. The other day a man was charged with striking a Socialist orator with an ice-pick. The judge lectured the orator on his Bolshevism, and then gave the accused imprisonment for a short term in the second division. Suppose that the Bolshevist had used an ice-pick on a Cabinet Minister!

I do not think that our judges and magistrates ever consciously show partiality. They are an upright class of men, men above suspicion. It is their unconscious that shows partiality, just as mine does. The army colonels who tried Conscientious Objectors were upright men, but it was wrong to imagine that they could possibly see the C.O.'s point of view. So it was with the regular R.A.M.C. doctors. To some of them the neurotic patient was a swinger of the lead, a malingerer. They had never heard of the new psychiatry, and the neurotic was a strange creature to them. Their ignorance supplemented their prejudice, and they could not possibly have treated these men with justice.

The truth is that we all make up our minds according as our buried complexes impel us. If I saw a Frenchman fighting a Scot I should take the Scot's side, because I have a Scot complex. Occasionally our complexes work in the opposite way. I fancy that the few people who sided with the Germans in the war were suffering from an "agin the government" complex, which, if you trace it deep enough is usually found to be an infantile rebellion against the father. In this case the State represented the father, and Germany was the outside helper who should conquer the father (or mother) country. Had Germany won, the unpatriotic man would immediately have turned his hate against Prussia, for then Prussia would have been the father substitute.

Our loves and hates and fears are within ourselves. I know a man who has a nagging wife; she has a constant wish for new things. He bought her a hat, and for two days she was happy; then she nagged, and he bought her a dress. Three days later she demanded a necklace, and he gave her a necklace. He may continue giving her everything she asks for, but if he buys her a Rolls Royce and a house in Park Lane she will be a dissatisfied woman, for "the fault, dear Brutus, lies not in our stars but in ourselves." I advised him to spend his money on having her psycho-analysed.

* * * * *

To-night Tammas Lownie the joiner came into Dauvit's shop. He is an infrequent attender at Dauvit's parliament, and Dauvit seemed slightly surprised at his entry.

"Weel, Tammas," he said, "it's no often that we see you here. What's brocht ye here the nicht?"

Tammas spat in the grate.

"Oh, it was a fine nicht, and I thought I'd just tak a daunder yont," he said easily.

Dauvit looked at him searchingly.

"Na, na, Tammas, it winna dae! It wasna the fine nicht that brocht ye yont. Ye've got some news I'm thinkin'."

Tammas laughed loudly.

"Dauvit, ye're oncanny!" he cried. "Ye seem to read what's at the back o' a man's held. But I have nae news to gie ye."

Dauvit chuckled.

"I wudna wonder if ye didna come yont to tell me aboot the eldership," he said slowly.

The expression on Tammas's face showed that he *had* come to tell us that the minister had asked him to become an elder.

"'Od, Dauvit, noo that ye come to mention it I wud like to hear yer advice aboot the matter. I dinna see how I can tak an eldership, Dauvit."

"How no?" asked Dauvit in surprise.

Then he added: "But maybe ye ken whether ye've got a sinfu' heart or no."

"It's no that," said Tammas hastily, "I'm nae worse than some other elders I ken," and he glanced at Jake Tosh. "No, it's no the sin I'm thinkin' o'; it's my trade."

"But," I put in, "why shouldn't a joiner be an elder?"

Tammas bit off a chunk of Bogie Roll.

"That may as may be, dominie, but I'm mair than a joiner; I'm an undertak-ker."

"Weel," said Dauvit, "what aboot that?"

Tammas shook his head sadly.

"An undertakker canna be an elder, Dauvit. Suppose the minister was awa preachin' or at the Assembly, and ane o' his congregation was deein', me as an elder micht hae to ging to the bedside and offer up a bit prayer."

"There's nothing in that," said Jake proudly; "I've offered up a bit prayer afore noo when the minister was awa."

"Aye, Jake," said Tammas, "but ye see you're a roadman. But an undertakker is a different matter. Goad, lads, I canna gie a man a bit prayer at sax o'clock and syne measure him for his coffin at acht. That wud look like mixin' religion wi' business."

The assembly thought over this aspect.

"All the same," said the smith, "Dr. Hall is an elder, and naebody ever thinks o' accusin' him o' mixin' religion wi' his business."

We all considered this statement.

"Tammas," said Dauvit, "if ye want to be an elder tak it, and never mind the undertakkin'. But if ever ye have to gie a prayer just get Jake here to tak on the job."

He began to laugh here.

"I mind o' Jeemie Ritchie when he got his eldership. The minister gaed awa to the Assembly in Edinbro, and as it happened auld Jess Tosh was deein', so Jeemie was asked to come up and gie her a prayer. Jeemie was in my shop when the lassie Tosh cam for him, and I never saw a man in sic a state.

"'Dauvit,' he cries, 'I canna dae it! I never offered up a prayer in my life!'

"'Hoots, Jeemie,' says I, 'it's easy; just bring in a few bitties frae the Bible.'

"Auld Jeemie he scarted his heid.

"'Man, Dauvit,' says he, 'I cudna say twa words o' the Bible.'

"Weel-a-weel, I had to shove him oot o' the shop, and I tell ye, boys, he was shakin' like a shakky-trummly.

"Weel, in aboot half-an-hour Jeemie cam back, and he was smilin' like onything.

"'Hoo did ye get on?' I speered.

"'Graund!' he cried, '. . . she was deid afore I got there!'"

*   *   *   *   *

When I published my *Log* a correspondent wrote accusing me of being disloyal to my colleagues in the teaching profession.

"Where is your professional etiquette?" he wrote.

I had lots of letters from teachers, some flattering, some not. One man wrote me from Croydon:—

"Dear Sir,—Are you a fool or merely a silly ass?"

"Both," I replied, "else I should not have paid 2d. for your letter."

In haste the poor man hastened to forward two penny stamps, and to apologise for not having stamped the letter he sent me.

"I really thought that I had stamped it," he wrote.

Then I wrote him a nice letter telling him that the mistake was mine, for his first letter had had a stamp on it after all. He never replied to that, and I suppose that now he goes about telling his friends that I am a fool, a silly ass, and a typical Scot.

Authors hear queer things about themselves. The other day a friend of mine asked for my *Log* in a West End library. As the librarian handed over the book she shook her head sadly.

"Isn't it sad about the man who wrote that book?" she said.

My friend was startled.

"Sad! What do you mean?"

"Oh, haven't you heard?" asked the librarian in surprise; "he's a confirmed drunkard now."

"Impossible!" cried my friend, "with whisky at ten and six a bottle!"

But I meant to write about colleagues. One day a class was holding a self-government meeting, and they sent for me. I was annoyed because I was having my after-dinner smoke in the staff-room. However I went up.

"Hullo!" I said as I entered, "what do you want?"

Eglantine the chairman said: "A member of this class has insulted you."

"Impossible!" I cried.

Then Mary got up.

"I did," she blurted out nervously; "I said you were just a silly ass."

"That's all right!" I said cheerfully, "I am," and I made for the door. Then the class got excited.

"Aren't you going to do anything?" asked Ian in surprise.

"Good Lord, no!" I cried. "Why should I?"

"You're on the staff," said Ian.

"Look here," I said impatiently, "I hereby authorise the crowd of you to call me any name you like."

The class became indignant.

"You can't criticise the staff," said one.

"Why not?" I asked, and they looked at each other in alarm. This was carrying self-government too far.

Suddenly Mary jumped up.

"Then if we can criticise the staff here goes! I accuse Miss Brown of favouritism."

It was a bombshell. Everyone jumped up, and some cried: "Shame! Withdraw!" The chairman appealed to me.

"I have nothing to do with it," I protested.

Then bitter words flew. They told me that I, as a member of the staff, should squash Mary. Voices became louder, but then the bell rang and the class had to go to its own class-room to work.

My colleagues when they heard the story agreed with the children; they held that I acted wrongly in listening to an accusation against a colleague. My argument was that I was a guest at a meeting; I had no vote, nor would I have interfered had I been a member of the meeting. I was quite sure that if the bell had not broken up the meeting somebody would have made the discovery that Miss Brown was the proper person to make the accusation to. When they thought that Mary insulted me they sent for me, and I fully expected they would send for Miss Brown. Again I argued that if Miss Brown had favourites the class had a right to criticise her. If she had no favourites let her arraign the class before a meeting of the whole school and accuse them of libel.

Looking back I still think my attitude was right, for unless the staff can lay aside all dignity and become members of the gang education is not free. Yet I see now that I was secretly exulting in the discomfiture of a colleague . . . a common human failing which none of us care to recognise in ourselves. It is a sad fact but a true one that however much Dr. A. protests when a patient tells him that Dr. B. is a clumsy fool, unconsciously at least Dr. A. is gratified at the criticism of his rival. Psycho-analysts, that is people who are supposed to know the contents of their unconscious, are just as guilty in this respect as other doctors, and if anyone doubts this let him ask a Freudian what he thinks of the Jungian in the next street.

My earliest memory of professional jealousy goes back to the age of seven. I lived next door to a dentist, a real qualified L.D.S. Across the street lived a quack dental surgeon. When trade was dull these two used to come to their respective doors and converse with each other in the good old simple way of putting the fingers to the nose. They never spoke to each other. Life in a northern town was simple in these days.

* * * * *

Helen Macdonald is four years old, and her mother and I have some breezy discussions about her upbringing. Mrs. Mac has a great admiration for her own mother, and she is bent on bringing up her daughter in the way that she was brought up.

"Mother made me obey and I'll make Helen obey," she said to-day with decision.

"It's dangerous," I said.

"No it isn't; it worked well enough in my case anyway."

"Don't blow your own trumpet, madam!"

She smiled.

"I don't think I am a bad product of the good old way," she said with a self-satisfied air.

"Madam, shall I tell you the truth about yourself?"

She bubbled and drew her chair closer to mine.

"Do!" she cried, and then added: "But I won't believe the nasty bits."

Mac chuckled.

"To begin with," I said pompously, "you are an awful example of a bad education."

She bowed mockingly and Mac guffawed. He is a wee bit afraid of his wife and he marvels at my courage in ragging her.

"You," I continued, "were made to obey as a child, and as a result you became dependent on your mother. In short you are your own mother."

"Don't be silly," she said with a frown; "I want your serious opinion."

"And you are getting it," I replied. "Because you had to obey you never lived your own life, and naturally you never had a mind of your own. To this day you act as your mother acted. She made her daughter obey; you follow her example; she made scones in such and such a way; you make scones in exactly the same way."

"That's right!" laughed Mac.

Mrs. Mac looked thoughtful.

"Anyway," she said quickly, "they are excellent scones."

"Most excellent scones," I hastened to add, "but my point is that if we all follow our parents there will be no progress."

"Progress will never bring better scones," said Mac and he patted his wife's cheek.

"Mac," I said gallantly, "your wife has brought scones to their perfect and utmost evolution. She has made the super-scone. Only, Helen isn't a scone you know."

At this point Helen was found trying to pull the marble clock down from the mantlepiece. Her mother rescued the clock as it was falling, and she scolded the fair Helen.

"You are all theory," she cried to me. "What would you do in a case like this?"

"Same as you did," I answered hastily, and then added: "Only I would try to give her so many interesting things to play with that she'd forget to want the clock."

Then Mrs. Mac indignantly dragged out Helen's toys from a cupboard.

"Dozens of them!" she cried, "and she is tired of every one."

Then I discoursed on toys. The toys of the world are nearly all bad. Helen has a beautiful sleeping doll that cost five pounds; rather I should say that Helen *had* a beautiful sleeping doll that cost five pounds. On the one occasion that Helen was allowed to play with it she made a careful attempt to open the head with a pair of scissors to see what made the eyes close and open. Then her mother put the doll in a box, packed the box in a trunk, and explained to Helen that the doll was to lie in that trunk until Helen had a little baby girl of her own.

I explained to Mrs. Mac that the toy a child needs is one that will take to pieces. Every toy should be a mine of discovery. The only good toys that I know of are Meccano and Primus, but there is much need for constructive toys for younger children.

"Mac," I said, "if you were even a passably good husband you would be making Montessori apparatus for your offspring."

We have many arguments like this. Mrs. Mac's problem is that of a million mothers; she has to fit the child into an adult environment. Yesterday she was painting in oils. The baker whistled outside and she ran out to get the bread. On her return she found that Helen was busily painting the pink wall-paper a prussian blue.

Wealthy mothers solve the problem by employing nurses, but the solution is a poor one. Few nurses know enough about children, and many do positive harm by frightening the child. Nor can the hired nurse give the infinite amount of love that a child demands. If she could it is probable that she would be sacked, for no mother likes to see her child lavish his love on another. On more than one occasion I have discovered that the parents of children who loved me were hostile to me. That is natural. If a father is continually hearing his daughter say: "Mr. Neill says this; Mr. Neill says that," I have every sympathy with him when he growls: "Damn this Neill blighter!" On the other hand I have no sympathy with him if he expects me to ask his little Ada how her dear charming papa is.

* * * * *

A book of ten volumes might well be written on the subject of parents and teachers. If a teacher were the author no publisher would look at it, for the language would be unprintable.

To the teacher the parent is an enemy. When Mrs. Brown comes to school she and the dominie chat pleasantly about the weather, while the children look on and marvel. Little Willie is amazed to see his mother smile as she talks, for it was only last night that he heard her say: "That Mr. Smith is by no means a gentleman. Did you see his nails?" Poor little Willie does not know that his mother and the dominie are using fair smiles to cover a real hostility. Mrs. Brown will talk agreeably all through her visit, but as she is shaking hands on the doorstep she will say, "Oh, by the way, Mr. Smith, Willie came home last night saying that he wasn't allowed to play hockey yesterday. I want him to play every Wednesday."

"But," says Mr. Smith deferentially, "I—er—well, Wednesday is the day when the Seniors play, and—er—since Willie is a Junior I—er—I—"

"Oh, thank you so much," she gushes, "I knew that you would arrange that he will play on Wednesdays," and she sails away.

Or perhaps Mrs. Brown will put it on to her husband.

"The way things are done at that school are disgraceful, Tom. You must go and see Smith and insist that the boy has his hockey."

Well, the poor father comes up to school, and he and the dominie discuss the weather and Lloyd George. All the time Brown is trying to muster up enough courage to tackle the hockey question.

"Er," he begins after clearing his throat, "my wife was saying something about—er—what a splendid view you have from here!"

"First rate," nods the dominie. "Your wife was saying?"

"Er—something about hockey." He coughs. "Splendid game! I—er—I must go . . . er—good-bye."

No mere man can badger a dominie.

From the parent's point of view a teacher is a rival when he isn't a sort of under-gardener. The parent would never think of arguing with the doctor when he says that Willie has measles; the doctor is a specialist in disease, and the parent is not. But it is different with the dominie. He is a specialist in education, but then so is the parent. That is possibly one of the reasons that the teaching profession is such a low-class one, for a teacher is merely a specialist in a world of specialists. Everybody knows how a child ought to be brought up. In justice to parents I must confess that there are only two teachers in Britain to whom I should trust the education of any child of mine. Most teachers are instructionists only, and the parent has some ground for suspicion.

X.

Duncan was talking about awkward moments to-night, and he told of the shock he got when he joined the army and found that the sergeant of his squad was an old pupil of his.

"I think I can beat that, Duncan," I said, and told him the story of an army lecture. I had a commission in the R.G.A. for a short time, and one morning I had to give a lecture to the men of the battery on lines of fire. They were mostly miners, and I tried to make the lecture as simple as possible. I began with the definition of an angle and went on to circular measurement. I noticed that one man stared at the blackboard in bewilderment, a very stupid looking fellow he was. When the lecture was over I approached him.

"I don't think you understood what I was trying to tell you," I said.

"I did have some difficulty in following it, sir," he said.

"H'm! What were you in civil life?"

"Mathematical master in a secondary school, sir."

I could not rise to the occasion. I fled to the mess and ordered a brandy and soda.

Speaking about rising to the occasion brings to my mind another army incident in which I did not shine. I was a recruit in the infantry, and a gym sergeant was putting us through physical jerks. He told us the familiar tale that although we had broken our mothers' hearts we wouldn't break his; in short he put the wind up us. I got very nervous.

"Right turn!" he roared, and I thought he said "Right about turn."

He told the squad to stand easy, and then he eyed me curiously.

"You! Big fellow! Take that smile off your face!"

I don't know why he said that for I couldn't have smiled at that moment for anything less than my ticket. He studied me carefully for a bit, then enlightenment seemed to dawn on him.

"I got it!" he exclaimed triumphantly.

"I know wot's wrong with you! You've got a stupid face; you can't think; you never thought in yer life."

I looked on the ground.

"*Did* yer ever think in yer life?"

"No, sergeant," I said humbly.

"I blinkin' well thought so!" he said and moved away.

Then the worm turned. Who was he that he should bully a scholar and a gentleman? I would lower him to the dust.

"Sergeant!"

He turned quickly.

"Wot d'ye want?" and he tried to freeze me with his look.

"It isn't my fault I can't think, sergeant; I was unfortunate enough to spend five years at a university."

His mouth gaped, and his eyes stared, but only for a moment. Then he rose to the occasion.

"I blinkin' well thought so!" he cried. "Squad! . . . . Tshun!"

* * * * *

It is Sunday night, and I have just been to town. At the Cross I stood and listened to a revivalist bellowing from a soap-box. His message was Salvation but I was more interested in the man than his message. Consciously he is out to save sinners, but I suspect that unconsciously he is out to draw attention to himself. I do not blame him. I do the same thing when I publish a book; Lloyd George and George Robey and the revivalist and I are all striving each in his little corner to draw attention to ourselves.

The exhibition impulse is in every child. A child loves to run about naked, but then society in the form of the mother steps in and says: "You must not do that!" But we know that every wish lives on in the depths of the mind, and the childish wish to exhibit the body appears in later years as a desire to preach or sing or act or lecture.

This is the psychology of the testimonials for liver pills which appear in every local paper. It is the psychology of much crime. Many a slum youth glories in having been birched, simply because his gang looks on him as a hero.

I hasten to state that exhibitionism alone does not make a Cabinet Minister or a comedian. There are other motives from infancy, an important one being the desire for power. I recall that as a boy I delighted in following a drove of cattle and smiting the poor creatures hard with a cudgel. Freud would say that in this way I was releasing sex energy, but I think that the infantile sense of power was at the root of my cruelty; here was I, a wee boy, controlling a big heavy stot. It is love of power that makes little boys want to be engine-drivers.

To the teacher this love of power is the most vital thing in a child's make-up. Discipline thwarts the boy at every turn, and our adult authority is fatally injuring the boy's character. Our task is to provide the child with opportunity to wield his power. We suppress it and the lad shows his power in destructive instead of constructive activities. I find that I keep returning to this subject of suppression, but it is the most important evil in education. It does not matter how perfect a teacher makes his instruction in arithmetic; if he has not come to see that suppression of a child is a tragedy, his instruction is of no value. From an examination point of view, yes; from a spiritual point of view, no.

* * * * *

Parents and teachers fail because they cannot see the world as the child sees it. The child of three is a frank egoist. He cares for no one but himself, and the world is his. Anger him and he would have you drawn and quartered if he had the power. His instincts prompt him to master his environment, and to begin with, when he is a few weeks old, his environment and his own person are indistinguishable.

Homer Lane gives a delightful description of the child's first efforts and how they are frustrated by ignorant adults.

"At a very early age the child becomes aware through various processes that his own hand which he has seen moving across his line of vision is a part of himself, and that he can move it himself. He has discovered power. He then enters upon his career. The same motive that will govern his behaviour for the rest of his life comes into operation, and he wants to use this new-found power for some purpose that will increase his enjoyment of life. Up to this time he has had only one pleasure, and that was to do with the commissariat. Having discovered power over his fist he therefore wants to put it in his mouth . . . a difficult task requiring much practice and patient perseverance.

"As he goes on working he learns that his power increases with effort, and now his motive is modified. At first it was purely materialistic; he wanted to have his fist in his mouth. Now he wants to put it there. His interest is in doing the thing rather than in having it.

"This is the spiritual element in his present desire, and now comes the first mistake in education. The mother, analysing the behaviour of the child, has noticed his complaint at the difficulty of the task as fatigue sets in, and, misunderstanding the motive of the child she helps him to put his fist in his mouth. But that is just what the child did not want, and he protests violently against this interference with his purpose in life.

"The mother again makes a false analysis of the situation, and concludes that his protest is the result of his disappointment that there is no nourishment in the fist. She then gives him food or paregoric, whatever may be her method of dealing with the spiritual unrest of her child, and thus drugs his creative faculties."

I have said that the infant is an egoist. If his egoism is allowed full scope he will enter upon the next stage of life, the self-assertive stage, with a huge capacity for being altruistic. This stage comes on about the age of six or seven. But if the child has had parents who believe in moulding character he will have had many severe lectures about his selfishness. These lectures will not have cured his selfishness; they will have driven it underground for the moment. The selfishness of adults is one result of the moral lecture in childhood, for no wish or emotion will remain buried for ever.

The age of self-assertion is the rowdy age, and naturally it is now that father uses his authority. The child is still ego-centric, but in a different way. At the age of three he was the king of the world; at the age of seven he is the king of the other boys who play with him. He is now reckoning with society, and he uses society as a background against which he may play the hero. Thus be bleeds Jack's nose for no reason in the world other than that he thus asserts himself. If he plays horses with the boy next door he insists upon being the driver.

It is at this period that he should be free from authority. If authority in the shape of father or teacher or policeman steps in to suppress his self-assertion the boy becomes an enemy of all authority and very often anti-social. The "rebel" in the Socialist camp is a good specimen of the man whose self-assertive period was injured by authority, and I suspect that the truculent drunk is letting off the steam that he should have let off at the age of eight.

The third stage in the evolution of a child is the adolescent stage. For the first time the boy becomes a unit in society. Hitherto he has played for his own hand; his games have been games in which personal prowess was the desired aim. Now he feels that he is one of a team. Even before puberty the team-forming impulse is seen; Puffer, for instance, in *The Boy and his Gang*, gives ten to sixteen as the gang age.

These divisions are purely arbitrary, and children differ much in evolution. The teacher, however, should have a general knowledge of these three phases. I have often seen a school prescribe cricket or hockey for boys who are still in the self-assertive stage. The result was that, having no team impulse, each boy had no further interest in the game when the umpire shouted: "Out!"

I used to umpire for boys and girls of eight to eleven, and it was a tiresome business. Quite often when a boy had been bowled with the first ball, he would throw down the bat in disgust and refuse to give the other side an innings. There was nothing wrong with the children; what was wrong was that a team phase game was being forced on a self-assertive phase group.

* * * * *

Duncan and two other dominies were in to-night and we got on to golf yarns. I remarked that there were very few good ones, and they all trotted out their favourites. I liked Duncan's best.

An oldish man was ploughing his way to the tenth hole at St. Andrews, and, when he ultimately holed out in nineteen, he turned to his caddie.

"Caddie," he cried in disgust, "this is the worst game I ever played."

The caddie stared at him open-mouthed.

"So ye *have* played afore, have ye?" he gasped in amazement.

Why are there no cricket or football stories, I wonder? Possibly because they are team games; a team is a crowd, and I never heard of a joke against a crowd. A crowd is an impersonal thing, and no one can joke about an impersonal thing. I never heard of a joke about the moon or a turnip. Yet are there not jokes against a nation, and a nation is a crowd? Take the joke about the Scot who was brought up at Bow Street for being drunk and disorderly. The magistrate, before passing sentence, asked the accused if he had anything to say for himself.

"Weel, ma lord, it was like this. I travelled frae Glesga to London yesterday, and I got into bad company in the train."

"Bad company?"

"Aye, ma lord. When I got into the train at Glesga Central I had twa bottles o' whuskey in my bag, and . . . a' the other men in my compartment was teetotal."

That looks like a joke against a long-suffering race, but is it so in reality? Make the traveller an 'Oodersfield' man on his way to see the Cup-tie Final at Chelsea, and it is not changed in essence. Only it has become a convention that the Scot is a hard drinker. It is the personal touch that makes the joke, and it is the individual that we laugh at.

I presume that the typical joke about Scots' meanness appeals to Englishmen because Englishmen are mean themselves. No joke appeals to a man unless it releases some repressed wish of his own. No one expects a devout Roman Catholic to see the point of a joke about extreme unction. The professional comedian to be a success must know what the crowd repressions are. Dickens is a great humorist because he knew by intuition what the crowd would laugh at. And that brings me to the subject of human types.

Broadly speaking there are two types of man. One is called an extrovert (Latin, to turn outwards); he identifies himself with the crowd, and he lives the life of the crowd. Lloyd George and Horatio Bottomley are typical extroverts; they seem to know instinctively what the crowd is thinking, and unconsciously they speak and act as the crowd wants them to speak and act. Dickens was another, and that is why he has so universal an appeal.

The other type, the introvert type, turns inward. They do not identify themselves with the crowd. What the public wants does not concern them; they give the crowd what they think it ought to want. This class includes the thinkers, the men who are in advance of their time. An introvert is never popular with the crowd because the crowd never understands him. He can never get away from himself, and he sums up events according to the personal effect they have on himself. Yet to the unconscious of the introvert crowd opinion is of the greatest importance.

In the realm of humour the extrovert is a success; what amuses him amuses the crowds. But the introvert laughs alone, and in some cases he decides that the crowd has no sense of humour, and he becomes a cynic.

It is necessary that the teacher should be able to recognise the different types. The extrovert is popular; he it is who leads the gang. Doubts and fears do not trouble him; life is pleasant and he laughs his way through it. But the introvert is the boy who stands apart in a corner of the playground; he is timid and fears the rough and tumble of team games. He feels inferior and he turns in upon himself to find superiority. Thus he will day-dream of situations in which he is a hero like David Copperfield when he stood at Dora's garden gate and saw himself rescuing her from the burning house.

I think that the job of the teacher is to help each type to a position midway between introversion and extroversion. The boy who lives in the crowd might well be tempted to take more interest in his own individuality, and the introvert might well be encouraged to project his emotions outward.

* * * * *

To-night Mac told me a story about old Simpson the dominie over at Pikerton. Last summer an English bishop was touring Scotland, and one morning he drove up to Simpson's school in a big car, flung open the door and walked in.

"Good morning, children," he cried.

The bairns sat gazing at him in awe. He turned to Simpson.

"My good sir," he protested, "when I enter a village school in England, the children all rise and say: 'Good morning, sir'!"

"Possibly," said Simpson dryly, "but in Scotland children are not accustomed to see strangers walk into a school. Scots visitors always knock at the door and await the headmaster's invitation to enter."

* * * * *

Mac and I were talking about education to-night.

"I never heard you mention the teaching side of education," he remarked. "Giving a child freedom isn't enough, you know. What about History and Geography and so on?"

"I think they are jolly well taught in many schools, Mac," I said. "It is the psychological side of education that is a thousand years behind the times."

"Yes," said Mac doubtfully, "but suppose you have a school of your own, I presume you'd teach the English yourself?"

I nodded.

"How would you do it?"

I thought for a while.

"I'd reverse the usual process, Mac," I said. "Usually the teacher begins with Chaucer and works forward to Dickens; I would begin with *Comic Cuts* and *Deadwood Dick* and work back to Chaucer."

"Oh, do be serious for once," he said impatiently.

"I am quite serious, Mac," I said. "The only thing that matters in school work is interest, and I know from experience that the child is interested in *Comic Cuts* but not in the *Canterbury Tales*. My job is to encourage the boy's interest in *Comic Cuts*."

I ignored Macdonald's reference to idiocy, and went on.

"You see, Mac, what you do is this: you see a boy reading *Deadwood Dick*, and you take his paper away from him and possibly whack the little chap for wasting his time. But you don't kill his interest in penny dreadfuls, and the result is that in later years he reads the Sunday paper that supplies the most lurid details of murders and outrages. My way is to encourage the lad to devour tales of blood and thunder so that in a short time blood and thunder have no more interest for him. The reason why most of the literature published to-day is tripe is that the public likes tripe, and it likes tripe because its infantile interest in tripe was suppressed in favour of Chaucer and Shakespeare."

"But," cried Mac, "isn't Shakespeare better for him than tripe?"

"Yes and no. If every poet were a Shakespeare the world would be a dull place; you need the tripe to form a contrast. The best way to enjoy the quintessence of roses, Mac, is to take a walk through the dung-heaps first."

"What books would you advise your pupils to read?" asked Mac.

"In their proper sequence . . . *Comic Cuts, Deadwood Dick, John Bull, Answers, Pearson's Weekly, Boy's Own Paper, Scout, Treasure Island, King Solomon's Mines, White Fang, The Call of the Wild, The Invisible Man,* practically anything of Jack London, Rider Haggard, Conan Doyle, Kipling."

"And serious literature?"

"All literature is serious, Mac."

"I mean Dr. Johnson, Swift, Bunyan, Milton, Dryden, and that lot," said Mac.

I smiled.

"Mac, I want you to answer this question: have you read Boswell's *Life of Johnson*?"

"Extracts," he admitted awkwardly.

"Bunyan's *Life and Death of Mr. Badman*?"

"No."

"Milton's *Areopagitica*?"

"Er—no."

"Swift's *Tale of a Tub*?"

"No."

I sighed.

"Would you like to read them?" I asked.

"I don't think they would interest me," he admitted.

"Then in heaven's name, why expect children to have any interest in them? If these classics weren't shoved down children's throats the adult population of this country would be sitting of an evening reading and enjoying Milton instead of *John Bull*."

Mac would not have this.

"Children must read the classics so that they may get a good style," he said.

"Style be blowed!" I cried. "The only way to get a style is by writing. Mac, I should cut out all the lectures about Chaucer and Spenser and Shakespeare, and let the children write during the English period . . . if I had periods, which I wouldn't. I don't want style from kiddies; I want to see them create in their own way. If they are free to create they will form their own style."

In a conversation one always has a tendency to overstate a case, and as the argument went on I found myself saying wild things. Writing calmly now I still hold to my attitude concerning style. I love a book written in fine style, but I refuse to impose style on children. In every child there is a gigantic protest. Thus the son of praying parents often turns out to be a scoffer. I had a good instance of the danger of superimposition of style.

I had a class of boys and girls of fifteen, sixteen, and seventeen years of age. For one period a week we all wrote five minute essays, and then we read them out. Sometimes we would make criticisms; for instance one girl used the word "beastly" in a serious essay, and we all protested against it. Then one day the head-master decided that they should write essays for him. He set a serious subject—The Function of Authority, I think it was—and then he went over their books with a blue pencil and corrected their spelling and style.

Three days later my English period came round. I entered the room and found the class sitting round the fire.

"Hullo!" I said, "aren't you going to write?"

"No," growled the class.

"Why not?"

"Fed up with writing. We want to talk about economics or psychology."

A fortnight later they made an attempt to write short essays, but it was a miserable failure; all the joy in creation had been killed by that blue pencil.

I can give an example of the other way, the only way. One boy of fifteen hated writing essays, and when I began the five minute essay game he sat and read a book. After a time I gave out the subject "Mystery," and I saw him look up quickly with flashing eyes.

"Phew! What a ripping subject!" he cried, "I must have a shot at that!"

His shot was promising, and he continued to make shots, until some of his essays were praised by the class. Then one day he came to me.

"I don't know anything about stops and things," he said, "and I want you to tell me about them."

This is my ideal of education; no child ever learns a thing until he wants to learn it. That lad picked up all he wanted to know about stops in half-an-hour. He was interested in stops because he wanted to write better essays. I need hardly say that he had listened to hundreds of lessons on stops during his school career.

* * * * *

To-morrow I return to London, and to-night I went over to say good-bye to Dauvit.

"Aye, dominie, and so ye're gaein' back to London!" he said.

"I don't want to leave this lazy life, Dauvit," I said, "but I must go back and start my school."

"It'll cost ye some bawbees to gang to London," put in Jake Tosh. "Penny three ha'pennies a mile noo-a-days I onderstand."

"A shullin' a mile for corps," remarked the undertaker.

Dauvit chuckled.

"So ye'll better no dee in London, dominie," he laughed.

"And that reminds me of Peter Wilson, him that passed into the Civil Service and gaed to London. He came hame onexpectedly wan mornin' and his father he says: 'What in a' the earth brocht ye hame in the month o' February, Peter? Surely ye dinna hae a holiday the noo?'

"'No,' says Peter, 'but I had a cauld and I thocht I was maybe takkin' pewmonia, and, weel father, corpses is a bob a mile on the railway.'"

"Dauvit," I said, "I don't care where I am buried."

"Is that so?" asked Jake in surprise. "What's become o' yer patriotism, dominie? I canna onderstand a man no wanting to be buried in his ain country. For my pairt I wudna like to be buried ony place but the wee kirkyaird up the brae there."

Dauvit grunted.

"What does it matter, Jake, whaur ye're buried?"

"Goad," said Jake, "it matters a lot. The grund up in the kirkyaird is the best grund in Scotland. It's a' sand, and they tell me that yer corp will keep for years in that grund."

Dauvit laughed, but the others seemed to take Jake's preservation argument seriously.

"Jake," said Dauvit, "does it no strike ye that to be buried in yer native place is a disgrace?"

"Hoo that, na?" said Jake.

"Because the man that bides in the place he was born in is of nae importance. A' the best men leave their native village, aye, and their native country. Aye, lads, the best men and the worst women leave their native country."

"I sincerely trust that you are not insinuating that they leave together, Dauvit," I put in hastily.

"No, they dinna do that, dominie; but whether they meet in London I dinna ken," and he smiled wickedly.

Jake spat in the grate.

"I dinna see what the attraction o' London is," he said with a touch of contempt.

"It is rather difficult to describe," I said. "For one thing you feel that you are in the centre of things. You are in the midst of all the best plays and concerts and processions . . . and you never think of going to see them. Then all the important people are there, the King and Lloyd George and Bernard Shaw . . . but you never see them anywhere. Then there are the places of historic interest, the Tower, Westminster Abbey, St. Paul's . . . and you don't know where they are until your cousins come up for a week's trip, and then you ask a policeman where the Tower is. And the strange thing is that you get to love London."

"There will be a fell puckle funerals I daresay," said the undertaker.

"To tell the truth," I answered, "I have never seen a funeral in London. In the suburbs, yes, but never in the centre of the West End. I've often seen them at the crematorium in Golders Green."

The undertaker frowned.

"That crematin' business shud be abolished by act o' Parliament," he said gruffly. "It's just a waste o' guid wood and coal. They tell me it taks twa ton o' coal ilka time."

I was surprised to find that the broad-minded Dauvit agreed with the undertaker in condemning cremation. I suspect that early training has something to do with it, and there may be an unconscious connecting of cremation with hell-fire. Dauvit's argument that cremation would destroy the evidence in poisoning cases was a pure rationalisation.

I wondered why the topic of funerals kept coming up, and I laughingly put the matter to Dauvit.

"Maybe it's because we're sad because ye're gaein' awa," he said half-seriously. "We'll miss yer crack at nichts."

At last I got up to go.

"Aweel, Dauvit, I'll be going," I said.

"Aweel, so long," said Dauvit without looking up. The others said "Guid-nicht" or "So Long," and I went out. I was sorry to leave these good friends, and they were sorry to lose me; yet we parted, it may be, for years, just as if we were to see each other to-morrow. We are a queer race.

XI.

When I arrived in London to-night I received a blow. A letter awaited me saying that the landlord of the school I was taking over had decided to sell the property. Thus all my dreams of a free school vanished in smoke. There isn't a house to rent in London; thousands are for sale, but I have no money to buy. If I had money I should hesitate to buy, for if a school is a success it expands, and the ideal thing to do is to take it out to the country where there is fresh air and space to grow.

To-night I feel pessimistic; it is difficult to be an optimist when a long-planned scheme suddenly falls to pieces.

I think of my capitalist friend Lindsay. He could buy me a school to-morrow, and never miss the money, but I don't think I should accept it. He would always have a big say in the running of it, and his ideals are not mine. I know other people with money, but I fancy that they have no faith in me. That is one of the disadvantages of writing light books like *A Dominie's Log*. The adult reads it and says: "Funny chap this!" But people have little faith in funny chaps. You can be a funny chap if you are a magistrate or a cabinet minister, but a teacher must be a staid dignified person. He must be a man who by his serious demeanour will impress the children and lead them out of the morass of original sin in which they were born. Montessori is catching on in the educational world not entirely because of her excellent system; part of her success is due to the fact that she never makes a joke; she is always the dignified moral model teacher.

Poor Montessori! Here I am transferring my irritation at the landlord who sold my school to her. I beg her pardon. Nor am I really annoyed with the landlord; the person I am annoyed with is myself. I bungled that school business.

Now I feel better. When I am irritated I always think of the traveller from St. Andrews. He arrived at Leuchars Junction and had five minutes to wait for the Edinburgh train. He entered the bar and had a drink. He had a second drink, and then awoke to the fact that he had missed the train. The next train was due in two hours. The barmaid shut the bar between trains and the traveller went out on the platform. It was a cold rainy November night. He went to the waiting room, but there was no fire there.

"Anyway," he said, "I'll have a smoke," and he filled his pipe. Then he found that he had but one match left. He struck it, and it went out. He went out to the platform and found an old porter screwing down the lamps. The porter knelt down to tie his lace and the traveller approached him.

"Could you oblige me with a match?"

The old porter eyed him dispassionately.

"I dinna smoke. I dinna believe in smokin.' I dinna hae a match."

The traveller walked wearily forward to an automatic machine and inserted his last penny . . . and drew out a bar of butterscotch. He tossed it over the line, and then he threw his pipe after it. He walked along the platform, and then he came back. The old porter was again tying his lace. The traveller suddenly rushed at him and kicked him as hard as he could.

"What did ye do that for?" demanded the poor old man when he picked himself up.

The traveller turned away in disgust.

"Och, to hell wi' you; ye're ay tying your lace!" he said.

Lots of people cannot see the joke in this yarn, and I challenge anyone to explain the point.

* * * * *

Good fortune came to rescue me from sorrowing over my lost school. It sent me to Holland thuswise: about five hundred Famine Area children were coming from Vienna to England, and I was invited to become one of the escort. Then it struck me that I might go over earlier and have a look at the Dutch schools. I hastened to get a few passport photographs; I looked at them . . . and then I thought I shouldn't risk going. However, on second thoughts, I decided to risk it, and went to the passport office. There a gentleman with a big cigar looked at the photograph; then he looked at me.

"The face of a criminal," his eyes seemed to say as he studied the photo.

"Isn't it like me?" I asked in alarm.

"Quite a good likeness," he said brusquely, and passed me on to the next pigeon-hole.

At last I landed in Flushing, and a kind guard found me a carriage. There I began to learn the Dutch language. "Niet rooken." Scots *reek* means *smoke*: hurrah! "do not smoke!"

"Verbodden te spuwen." "It is forbidden to——" no, that wouldn't be nice! Got it! "Do not spit!"

At this juncture a pretty Scheveningen lassie entered and greeted me. Alas! I knew but five words of Dutch, and when I thought the matter over I concluded that they were not very appropriate for carrying on a mild flirtation. Still, it's wonderful how much you can do with facial expression. Just before the train started a man entered. He knew English, and with more kindness than knowledge of humanity he offered to act as interpreter. The ass! as if a fellow can tell a girl through an interpreter that her hair is just the shade he admires. This fisher lassie was the only pretty girl I saw in Holland in ten days.

Rotterdam. My first and abiding impression was that never before had I seen so many badly-dressed people. If I had money and a profiteering complex I should set up a Bond Street shop in the centre of Rotterdam. No, that's wrong; that wasn't my first impression at all: my first impression was of a window filled with cigars at six cents each—one and a fifth pence. From that moment I loved Holland and the Dutch. What did it matter if their clothes were badly cut? What did anything matter? I dived into that shop and bought twenty . . . and ten yards farther on discovered a shop with fatter and longer cigars at five cents each. Three days later in the Hague I walked round the cigar shops for two hours, dying for a smoke, but not daring to buy a cigar at five cents lest in the next street I should find a shop offering them at four cents.

It was in Rotterdam that I discovered how bad my manners were. I was sitting in a cafe when a gentleman entered. He swept off his hat and bowed graciously . . . and I hastily put a protecting hand on the pocket containing my pocket-book. But every man who entered greeted me in the same way, and I realised that I was in a polite country. By the end of the week I was beating the Dutch at their own game, for I swept off my hat to every policeman, shopkeeper, tramwayman I spoke to.

On a Monday morning I walked forth to inspect the Dutch schools. I saw a troop of little girls following a mistress, and I joined the procession. They turned into a playground, and I followed. I approached the lady.

"Do you speak English?"

"Engelish! Ja!" she said with a smile.

"I am an English—no, Scots teacher," I explained, "and I should like to see the school."

"I will ask the head-mistress," she said, and entered the school, while I stood and admired the bonny white dresses of the girls.

She returned shaking her head.

"The head-mistress says that it is not allowed to visit a school in Holland without a permit from the Mansion House."

"A rotten country!" I growled, and went away.

In the street I ran into a group of boys led by a master who was smoking a fat cigar.

"Speak English?" I asked, lifting my hat gracefully.

"Nichtenrichtilbricht," he said; at least that's how it sounded.

"Thank you," I said, lifted my hat again, and fell in behind the boys. I was determined to see this thing through.

I tackled him again when we reached the playground.

"I the head would see," I began, "the ober-johnny, the chef."

"Ja!" he exclaimed with an enlightened grin, and nodded. In ten seconds the chief stood before me. He could speak a broken English, and said he would be glad to show me round. It was a third class school, and I gathered that in Holland there are three grades of State school; the first class is attended by the rich, the second by the middle class, and the third by the poor.

The school was very like a Board School in England. The children sat in the familiar desks and were spoon-fed by the familiar teacher. There was nothing new about it. I noticed that hand writing seemed to be the most important thing, and each class teacher proudly showed me exercise books filled with beautiful copper-plate writing. Most obliging class teachers they were. Would I like to hear some singing? It was wonderful singing in three parts; what surprised me was that the boys seemed to be just as keen on singing as the girls. I have always found it otherwise in Scotland and England.

In this school I got the gratifying news that corporal punishment is not allowed in Dutch schools, and later I learned that this applies to all reformatories also.

I think the Dutch are fond of children. Children seem to be everywhere. I went to the police-station to register as an alien, and as the inspector was examining my passport his wee girl of three toddled in and climbed on his knees. He laid down his pen and fondled the child. Then his wife came in; she had been out shopping, and wanted him to admire the big potatoes she had bought. I was delighted to see the human element mingle with the official. A country that allows wives and children to mix up with its red-tape is on the right road to health if not wealth.

I went to the Hague next day, and English friends met me at the station and piloted me to their home. Next morning I visited an establishment called the Observatiehuis, and found that the superintendent had spent six years in England and had an English wife. The observation house, he explained, is a home for bad boys. When convicted they are sent there and are "observed." If a boy is well-behaved he is sent to live with a family and learn a trade; if he is incorrigible he is sent to a reformatory.

I looked in vain for the new psychological way of treating delinquents. There was discipline here, but it was kindly discipline, for Mr. Engels is a kindly man; the boys sang as they swept the stairs. That was good, yet, it was Mr. Engels that brought freedom into the school; his successor may be a bully.

From Mr. Engels I got a letter of introduction to a real reformatory in Amersfoort, and off I set. Amersfoort is inland and I expected to find much language difficulty there, for I thought it unlikely that English would be spoken so far inland.

Amersfoort is a beautiful old town, and I at once set out to find the Coppleport mentioned in my guide-book. I suppose I looked a lost soul. A youth of eighteen jumped off his cycle and lifted his cap. Then he pointed to a badge he wore in his coat.

"Boy scout!" he said.

"Excellent!" I cried, "you speak English?"

He held out his hand.

"Good bye!" he said; "pleased you to meet!"

"How do you do?" I said.

He grinned.

"God damn!" he said sweetly.

After that conversation seemed to die down. I managed to convey to him that I was looking for the Coppleport, and he led me to it. Gradually his English improved, and he told me of his brother in England. A nice lad. I told him that I had once had a long conversation with the great B.P., but he looked blank.

"Baden Powell, your chief," I explained.

He shook his head; he had never heard of B.P. I think now that what was wrong was that he did not understand the name as I pronounced it; possibly he knows B.P. under the sound of Bahah Povell or something similar.

On the following morning I went to the reformatory. It was a beautiful building fitted with every appliance necessary . . . and one not necessary—a solitary confinement room. A young teacher, Mr. Conijn, a very decent chap, who could speak excellent English, showed me round. Every door we came to had to be opened with a key and locked behind us. Here there was more of military discipline than in the Observatiehuis, but none of the boys looked sulky or unhappy. The relations of the boys and the teachers were fine; as Conijn passed a lad he would pull his hair or pass a funny remark, and the boy would grin and reply.

"Any self-government?" I asked.

"We tried it but it was no good. It may work with English boys but not with Dutch," said Mr. Conijn.

"Did you have locked doors?" I asked.

"Oh, yes."

"Then self-government hadn't the ghost of a chance to succeed," I remarked.

We entered a class where an old man of about eighty was teaching a group.

"Why do these lads keep their eyes on the ground?" I asked. "Is their spirit crushed out of them?"

Conijn laughed.

"They are admiring your boots!" he cried.

I wore a pair of ski-ing boots on my trip, and all Holland stared open-mouthed at them. If I had been wanted for a murder I don't think anyone in Holland could have identified me, for their eyes never got above my boots.

One of the masters, Mr. van Something-or-other, very trustingly lent me his bike, and on the following day I cycled to Laren to see the Humanitarian School there. Nearly every road has a cycle path on one side and a riding path on the other, but in spite of the excellent roads I did not enjoy cycling in Holland; a free wheel was of little value on the flat surface. One delightful feature about cycling in Holland is that there are no mid-day closing times for pubs, but on the other hand you cannot raise much of a thirst in a flat country.

Well, I reached Laren after many narrow escapes, for I was continually forgetting that you keep to the right in Holland. A postman came along, and I jumped off.

"Humanitaire School?" I asked as I doffed my hat.

By his expression I judged that he did not know the institution under that name.

"School," I said, and he nodded and pointed to the village State school.

"Nay! School Humanitaire!" I persisted.

At this juncture another man came forward, and the two of them jawed away gutturally for some time. I began to grow weary.

"Hell!" I murmured to myself half aloud.

The postman brightened, and enlightenment came to him.

"Engelissman!" he exclaimed.

"Liar!" I cried, "I'm a Scot," and I left the two of them discussing Engelissmen.

After much trouble and many bitter words I found the school. A gentleman who looked extremely like Bernard Shaw before Shaw's hair turned grey, was digging in a garden with a lot of boys and girls. He was Mr. Elbrink, the head-master. He could speak English and he showed me round.

The school is rather like what is known as the crank school in England. In a manner it is the super-crank school, for everyone on the staff is teetotal, vegetarian, and a non-smoker. Here it was that I heard of Lightheart for the first time, and I blushed for my ignorance of the gentleman. It appears that he was a great educational reformer, a sort of Froebel I fancied, for handwork seemed to be the main consideration in the school. But I regret to say that the school did not impress me much. Too many children were doing the same sort of work; they sat in desks and held themselves more or less rigid. Here was benevolent authority again, not true freedom. All schools in Holland are State schools, and the Humanitarian School is one of them. It is almost impossible for a State school to be very much advanced; I think it is impossible, for the State is the national crowd, and a large crowd has little use for the crank.

I returned to Amersfoort, where by this time I had become the guest of the International School of Philosophy. This is a building standing in about twenty acres of ground amid the pine forests two miles south of the town. I was the sole guest, for the summer classes had not started. This school is the beginning of a great movement. Here students from every country will meet and discuss life and education. Mr. Reiman, the president, talked long and earnestly to me about the scheme, but I found myself challenging his insistence on spiritual education.

The aim of the school is to develop the spiritual side of man, an excellent aim . . . so long as man does not imagine that by living on the higher plane he is annihilating his earthly self. Everyone there was very, very kind to me, but I did not feel quite in my element, for I am not an obviously spiritual person. I find that I can discuss the higher life best when I have a glass of Pilsener at my elbow and a penny cigar in my mouth. It is clear that I have a complex about the higher life, and it may be a sour-grapes complex. All the same I should like to attend a summer course at Amersfoort and listen to the wise men dilate on the Bhagavadgita, Psycho-analysis and Religion, Plato, Sufism, and other subjects on the programme; anyway I would have no prepossessions and prejudices in listening to Dr. G. R. S. Meads' course of lectures on The Mystical Philosophy and Gnosis of the Trismegistic Tractates.

From Amersfoort I went to Amsterdam.

"Umsterdum, dree klasse, returig," I said to the ticket office girl.

"Third class return?" she asked with a smile and gave me the ticket.

I was indignant.

It is the most humiliating thing in the world to ask a question in Dutch and to be answered in English. In Rotterdam I had stopped a seafaring looking man and tried to ask him in Dutch what was the way to the Hotel de France. He listened patiently while I struggled with the language; then he spat on my boot.

"Hotel de France?" he replied in broad Cockney, "damned if I know."

On the way to Amsterdam I got into a carriage full of farmers and one of them made a remark to me. I shook my head.

"Engelissman?" he said.

I nodded.

Then those men began to talk about Engelissmen, and they talked and laughed all the way to Amsterdam. Every now and then one of them would jerk his thumb in my direction. It was a trying journey.

Arrived in Amsterdam I made for the Rijks Museum. At the door a seedy-looking man touched me on the arm.

"Guide, sir?"

"No thank you."

"Two hundred rooms, sir! Official guide."

"No thank you."

He kept pace with me, and in a weak moment I inquired his charge. It was three guilden (five shillings), and I saw at once that the dirty dog had won, for he took on an air of possession.

"Righto," I said resignedly, and he led me into the building.

He began his tiresome patter.

"Thees picture was painted in 1547; beautiful ees eet not? Wonderful arteest!"

I sighed.

"Take me to the Rembrandts," I said.

I cannot describe this incident. I hated the beast because I had been so weak as to accept his services. The beauty of Rembrandt and Franz Hals was lost on me; all I could see was the dirty face of that guide. Rembrandt's *Night Watch* made me forget the creature for a moment, but when he began to describe it I fled in horror. We finished up in the modern section, and as I looked at van Gogh and Cézanne and Whistler's *Effie Deans* his squeaky voice kept up a running commentary. I rushed from the building after a ten minutes' tour, paid the worm his three guilden . . . and then went back and enjoyed the gallery. But I nearly committed murder in the Rijks Museum that day. If ever I am hanged it will be for murdering an official guide. This particular specimen spoiled my visit to Amsterdam. I could not get away from the thought of my weakness, and I fled the city.

In the train going back to Amersfoort a genial Dutchman made a remark to me. I resolved that I should pretend to be a fellow-countryman.

"Ja!" I said, and the answer seemed to satisfy him. He went on to say other things, and when his facial expression seemed to demand an affirmative I said "Ja!"

After a time he frowned as he said a sentence.

"Nay!" said I.

That did it. He became white with anger, and swore at me all the way to Amersfoort. He had a fine command of language, too, and I was extremely sorry that I could not understand it.

On the Saturday I set off on my return journey to Rotterdam, doing a tour in American fashion of Leiden on the way. It was like going home, for I liked Rotterdam. I think it was the gay paint on the barges that attracted me so much.

On the Sunday morning the Austrian kiddies arrived, and my sight-seeing ended.

XII.

The Austrian kiddies arrived at the Maas station on Sunday morning, and the Dutch folk gave them a kindly welcome. The Rotterdam committee was in charge, and I stood back because it was not my job. The kiddies came tumbling out of the train with great relief, for they had travelled for two nights. All had heavy rucksacks, many of them the packs of their dead fathers and brothers.

My eye lit on little Hansi. She stood on the platform crying, and I went forward to comfort her. Alas! I knew less German than I did Dutch, and I knew not what she said; but one of the Austrian escort told me that she had been homesick all the way. There is, however, a universal language that all children understand, and I took wee Hansi in my arms and cuddled her. The flow of tears stopped and she took from a small basket slung to her neck a tiny naked doll. I included Puppe in the cuddle, and Hansi smiled. A dear wee mite she was, very very thin, with great big eyes that were sunken. Her tears did not affect me, but when she smiled I found myself weeping, and I had to blow my nose hard.

The four hundred and fifty-eight children were bundled across the road to a ship, which took them in two parts across the Maas to the large building used by the Cunard Line for emigrants. Many of them thought they were on the way to England, and ten minutes later I found a wee chap gazing round in wonder on the land of England.

"This aint England, anywye," he said at last in evident disgust; "look at them clogs! This is Holland."

The boy was a Londoner resident in Vienna. There were about a dozen English children in the party. Later I found one standing in front of a group of Austrian boys.

"Any one o' you," he was shouting, "I'll box the whole gang o' you!"

This Cockney, his little brother, and their sister were the thorn in the flesh of the escort.

"Absolute terrors," declared everyone, but I liked them.

Many of the children were middle class, children of doctors, lawyers, architects, and so on; nice kiddies they were. The bigger girls could speak English, and I used them as interpreters.

On the Monday morning the English escort took charge. The first task was medical inspection, and the two English doctors and four or five Dutch doctors prepared for action. Our job was to marshal the kiddies, help them to take their shirts off, and then bundle them into the inspection room. It sounds easy, but it was a weary business. You looked down the list for No. 258, and you found a name.

"Mitzi Dvoracek!" you called, and wondered whether a boy or a girl would appear. There was no answer . . . and an hour later you found a little girl who had lost her identity card, and you concluded that she was Dvoracek, but she wasn't; her name was Leopoldine Czsthmkyghw, or something resembling that.

I was greatly troubled by their questions. Following a method I had used with indifferent effect while conversing with garrulous Dutchmen in railway carriages, I answered "Ja" and "Nay" alternately. Many of the children stared at me in wonder and I marvelled . . . until I discovered that most of them had been asking me the way to the lavatory. After that I just pointed to a door in the wall when a boy asked me a question, and when one lad didn't seem to understand, I took him by the back of the neck and shoved him through the door. Then I found that he had been asking the time.

I gave up replying to questions after that.

The children had all been examined, and one lad stood alone; he had no card and no one could place him. Then he confessed that he was a stowaway who had been too old to join the batch, and had boarded the train quietly at Vienna. Mrs. Ensor, the secretary of the Famine Area Committee, proved herself a sport by declaring that she would take him to England. The good Dutch folk also rose to the occasion, and went out and bought him a pair of short trousers.

In the afternoon I sat down beside a few boys. And then I did a fatal thing. A boy dropped his pencil and I picked it up, threw it over the house . . . and then produced it from another lad's pocket. That did it. In two seconds I had a hundred children round me roaring at me. An Austrian lady explained that they were calling me a magician and asking for more. I blushingly told her to explain to them that it was my only trick. Sighs of disgust followed, and I was on the point of losing my popularity when I hastily got the lady to explain to them that I had a better talent . . . I could make anyone laugh merely by looking at him. Fifty of them at once challenged me to begin, and I had a great time. One lad beat me, but then he had toothache, a blistered heel, and was homesick.

After a time I asked them to sing to me, and they sang sweet folk songs of their home. They were delightful singers, and the boys sang as eagerly and as well as the girls. In England boys usually hate singing. I marvelled at their all knowing the same songs, and one of the girls explained to me that in Austria every school has the same songs; more than that, every school has the same class-books, and if two children living a hundred miles apart meet on the street they can say to each other: "I'm at page 67 of my Geography. What page are you at?"

They demanded a song from me, and I sang *Now is the Month of Maying*, and, by special request, *Tipperary*. Then I asked them to sing their National Anthem, and the lady began it, but the children did not follow her. At my look of surprise the lady said: "They cannot sing it because now they feel that they have no Austria left to sing about."

A man's voice sounded from inside the building, and they rushed indoors, for it was the voice of their beloved Ministry of Health doctor, who had brought them from Vienna, and they all loved him. They forgot me at once and left me . . . all but one. Little Hansi put her wee hand in mine and snuggled closer . . . and that's why I love her so very much.

On Tuesday morning they all took up their packs, and we set off for England via the Maas boat and station. We packed into carriages and set off. There was no water on the train, but we laughed and said: "We'll be in Flushing in two hours! We are a special!" We were. We left the Maas station at one o'clock, and we travelled until three. Then we drew up . . . and found we were back at the Maas station. Where we had been I don't know, but it was the biggest mystery of my life. Well, we crawled along past picturesque villages where women with white caps and red arms smiled on us and gave us water to drink. And at eight o'clock we reached Flushing all very weary and extremely dirty. The kiddies had a good meal set out on white tablecloths, and the doctor and I had the best Pilsener of our lives. We handed over the kiddies to the ship stewards and the fresh escort from England, and retired to rest.

I awoke at six and found that all the children were on deck, and the bad English boy almost in the water, for his heels were off the ground and his head far down towards the water. He was looking for fish, he said. None of the children had seen the sea before, but I think they were too tired to be excited about it. They did become excited when they saw the cliffs of Dover.

Much to my annoyance a gentleman had been teaching them *God Save the King* on the way over. I was annoyed because I knew it was a piece of jingoism meant for the journalists at Folkestone. When we drew up at the pier, sure enough the gentleman struck up the tune, and the kiddies sang it. But the girls who could speak English sang *God Save YOUR Gracious King*. I thought it a beautiful touch; the finest piece of good taste I have ever come across.

I didn't like the well-dressed ladies who came bossing around at Folkestone. Frankly I was jealous. As I was leading the children off the steamer, one of them touched me on the arm and asked me to make way for the children. And I smiled to see that the women in rich dresses managed somehow to get in front of the camera.

We took the children to Sandwich by rail and then to a camp by motor lorry. It was a tiresome job loading and unloading the lorry, but after six trips I found that every child was in camp. I went off to have a wash and some tea, and then, glowing with self-satisfaction at all I had done, I lit a cigar and walked outside. A gentleman passed me.

"Are you a worker?" he demanded.

"I—er—I suppose I am—in a way," I said modestly.

"Well, don't you think you might find something to do?" he asked. "There's plenty to do, you know."

Then for the first time in my life I understood the old Mons Ribbon men who used to annihilate the recruit with the terse phrase: "Afore you came up!"

The pressmen passed by, a dozen of them with the stowaway in their midst. Presently they posed him and a dozen cameras snapped while a cinema burred. And next day the papers told a romantic story; the stowaway had crept into the train at Vienna, and, foodless, had hid until he arrived in Rotterdam. Then darkly he had crept on board the ship and had been discovered at Folkestone. Also when next day I saw in the pictorial papers a photograph of a boy violinist playing to his chums, I was not very much surprised to find the title of the photo was: *The Stowaway Entertains His Companions*. As a matter of fact, the fiddler wasn't the stowaway at all, but this incident makes me think hard about history. If a Fleet Street reporter changes one boy into another, why, we may be all wrong in our history. Henry VIII. may only have had one wife, and the reporter who interviewed him may have had so much sack to drink that his vision along with the journalistic touch may have manufactured the other five. The tale of King Harold being shot through the eye at the Battle of Hastings may have arisen from a reporter's using the figurative expression that William the Conqueror "put his eye out." Nor, after reading the account of the landing of the Austrian children, can I believe the tale of the minstrel Taillifer who sprang into the water to lead the Normans in landing. And as for the time-honoured phrases, "Take away that bauble!" and "England expects every man to do his duty," I don't believe they were ever uttered—not now.

I am not singling out journalists as special misreporters. Not one of us can report an incident truly. There is a good example of this truth in Swift's *Psychology and Everyday Life*, just published. Swift prepared a stunt as a test for his adult class. In the midst of a serious lecture two men and two women students created a disturbance outside in the lobby, then they burst into the room. One held a banana pistol-wise at another's head. Swift dropped a toy bomb, and one of the students staggered back crying: "I'm shot!"

One student dropped a parcel containing a brick, and all yelled and made much noise. The class was seriously alarmed until they were assured that the whole affair was a put-up job. Each student was asked to write an account of what had happened, and the result of their attempts is so astounding that the reader becomes uncertain whether any witness in a law-court ever tells the truth. Few, if any, students could identify one of the wranglers; every account said that the banana was a real pistol; only one or two saw the brick drop. The strangest thing was that many were quite sure of the identity of the actors . . . and one or two of the accounts named students who had long since left the college. I write from memory, but the facts were as arresting as the ones I have given.

This makes one uneasy about the methods the police adopt to identify a prisoner. If I saw a man shoot another in Piccadilly, it is a thousand to one chance that I should not be able to identify him later. Yet many a man has been hanged on identification.

But I meant to finish my account of the Austrian kiddies. The time came when I had to leave them and return to London. I set out to find my Hansi to say good-bye to her. I saw her in the distance . . . and then I ran away, for I hate saying good-bye.

I liked those kiddies, dear wee souls, just as sweet as any English kiddies, but then children have no nationality; they are lovable for they all belong to the Never Never Land. Barrie proved himself a genius when he created Peter Pan, for Peter symbolises man's highest wish—to become a little child and never grow up. "Genius," he says, "is the power of being a boy again at will." It is true in his case. Yet this kind of genius is retrospective; it is a regression. The genius who will help man to look forward instead of backward must not return to boyhood; he must go forward to superman. To put it psychologically, Barrie's genius comes from the unconscious, but what the world needs is a man whose genius will come from the superconscious, the divine.

XIII.

I have just been reading Jack London's *Michael, Brother of Jerry*, and I am full of righteous rage. What a picture! It is the story of how performing animals are trained, and before I had read half the book I made a vow that never again will I sit through a performance of animals.

The tale of Ben Bolt the tiger, if known by the masses, would kill every animal turn on the stage. Ben Bolt, fresh from the jungle, is broken by the trainers. The method is unspeakable; he is lashed with iron bars and stabbed with forks until in agony he falls senseless in the arena. This treatment goes on for weeks . . . and in the end many good, kindly people see Ben Bolt, a miserable, broken animal, sit up in a chair like a human. And they laugh. My God!

Then there is Barney the good-natured mule that was once a family pet. Later he becomes the celebrated bucking mule, and a prize is offered to anyone who will keep on his back for one minute. Audiences go into fits of laughter at his antics. But the audiences do not know that Barney was trained with a spiked saddle, and that for months life was one long agony of pain.

Is my anger due to the cruelty I am repressing in myself? I don't care whether it is sadism or the spark of the divine in me. All I care about is that this inferno of pain must cease.

Never has any book affected me as this one has done. By word of mouth and by my pen I shall try my hardest to send dear old Jack London's message round the world. Public opinion is the only thing that can stop the misery of these broken creatures, and I suggest that the anti-vivisectionists turn their energies to this infinitely worse evil. The vivisectionists, at any rate, are working for humanity, but the brutes who break performing animals are merely amusing crowds of good people who know nothing about what goes on behind the scenes.

* * * * *

I see in the newspaper that Mary Pickford and Douglas Fairbanks held up the traffic in Piccadilly. They appeared on a balcony at the Ritz, and the crowd went frantic. The super-hero and the super-heroine of the cinema drew the crowd's emotion to them, and Tagore the Indian poet arrived in town at the same time unnoticed. It would seem that the crowd responds to the presence of the unimportant person only. London went mad over Hawker and Jack Johnson, and Georges Carpentier; and if Charlie Chaplin were to come over, I fancy London would take a general holiday.

No one will contend that these people are of supreme importance in the scheme of life. Charlie is a funny little man; Douglas Fairbanks is a fine lump of a fellow; Mary Pickford is a sweet little woman. But Tagore will live longer; Thomas Hardy, Bernard Shaw, Bertrand Russell, Sigmund Freud are of greater moment to humanity, yet each could walk out of Paddington Station and be unrecognised by the crowd.

The morning paper shows well that the crowd is interested only in unessentials. "Punish the profiteers!" was the press cry a few months ago. Well, they punished the profiteers . . . and prices continued to rise. A few years ago the cry was: "Flog the white slave traffickers!" They flogged them, and yet I still see thousands of white slaves in the West End of London. And while Europe is sinking into anarchy and bankruptcy to-day, the only remedies the crowd representatives—the press—can think of are remedies of the Hang-the-Kaiser type. I believe that the crowd still thinks that juvenile crime is mainly caused by cinema five-part dramas.

The crowd is rather like the individual unconscious; it is primitive, and like the unconscious it can only wish. The crowd that welcomed Mary and Douglas was closely akin to the personal unconscious. Douglas stands to each individual in the crowd as the eternal hero, the man who always wins. Each man in the crowd sees in Douglas his own ideal self, so that when the office boy cheers Douglas he is cheering himself. Mary has been well named "the world's sweet-heart"; she is the ideal heroine, beautiful, wronged, protected by six foot of masculinity. Both come from the world of make-believe, the world of phantasy. Their arrival in England simply made a dream come true.

Now I am certain that if any individual in the great Piccadilly crowd had met Douglas and Mary on the boat, he or she would have looked at them with interest, but there would have been no cheering and throwing of roses. What the crowd does is to raise an emotion to a superlative degree. In a full hall you will laugh at a joke that would not bring a smile to your face in a room. You become absorbed in your crowd, and you are fully open to your crowd's suggestion. I generally laugh at Charlie Chaplin, but one night a cinema manager, a friend of mine, gave me a private view of Charlie's latest production. I sat alone in the large cinema palace . . . and I couldn't even smile. Had a crowd been there to share my laugh, I should have roared.

The Douglas-Mary episode makes me pessimistic about the future of democracy. For democracy is crowd rule, and the crowd is a baby when it isn't a savage. Yet we have no real democracy in this country. We have a slave state, the exploiters and the exploited, the "haves" and the "have nots." Douglas and Mary came over, and the poor beauty-starved populace forgot for the moment its poverty, and showered all its pent-up emotion on the people from picture-book land.

In Elizabethan times the world was a place of wonder; every mariner was coming home with wondrous tales of Spanish gold and men with necks like bulls. All you had to do to find a reality that was more wonderful than fancy was to sail away across the sea. But to-day the world holds no mystery; there are no pirates to overcome, no prisoned maidens to rescue. Reality means toil and taxes and trouble. But there is a land where men are dew-lapped like bulls . . . the land of phantasy. There is a society where the villain always gets his deserts . . . the land of film pictures. And when your hero and heroine walk out of the picture and become real flesh and blood, what are you to do? After all, you cannot pour all your emotion into your looms and office-desks and counters. Sweet-faced Mary does not know it, but she is one of the best allies that our capitalist system could have; for if the crowd were not showering its emotion on her it might well be using it up in the smashing of all the ugly things in our civilisation.

* * * * *

I have been thinking of the crowd in another aspect. Last year in a merry mood I sat down to write a novel. I meant it to be a comedy, but, having no control over the characters, I found that they insisted in making the story a farce. The result was *The Booming of Bunkie*. I thought it a very funny book, and I laughed at some of my own jokes and murmured, "Good!" I impatiently awaited the book's appearance, and when the day of publication came I sat down hopefully to await the press notices. The first one to come in was lukewarm.

"Why do papers send a funny book to an old fossil of a reviewer with no sense of humour?" I said, testily and waited for the next post. Well, it came; it brought three adverse notices and a letter.

"Dear Dominie, I admired your *Log*, but why, oh why, did you perpetrate such a monstrosity as *The Booming of Bunkie*?"

Then a friend wrote me a letter.

"Dear old chap,—You are suffering from the effects of the war. If the war has induced you to write *Bunkie*, I am all for hanging the Kaiser."

For weeks I clung to the belief that the crowd had no sense of humour . . . then I re-read my novel. I still hold that it is funny in parts, but I see what is wrong. It is a specialised type of humour, or rather wit, the type that undergraduates might appreciate. In fact I was recently gratified to hear that the students of a Scots university were rhapsodising about it. The real fault of the book is that it is clever, and to be clever is to be at once suspect.

I naturally like to think that the circulation of a book is generally in inverse proportion to its intrinsic merit. J. D. Beresford's novels are, to me, much better than those of the late Charles Garvice, yet I make a guess that Garvice's circulation was many times greater than Beresford's. Still I cannot argue that the reverse is true—that because a book does not go into its second edition it is necessarily good. I find that the problem of circulations is a difficult one. I cannot, for instance, understand why *The Young Visitors* sold in thousands; I failed to raise a smile at it. Again, there is my friend although publisher, Herbert Jenkins. I didn't think *Bindle* funny, yet it has been translated into umpteen European languages. Jenkins himself does not think it funny, and that, possibly, is why he is my friend.

The most surprising success to me was Ian Hay's *The First Hundred Thousand*. I read Pat MacGill's *Red Horizon* about the same time, and thought Hay was stilted and superior with a public-school man's patronising Punch-like attitude to the working-class recruits. I thought that he didn't know what he was writing about, that he had not reached the souls of the men. MacGill, on the other hand, gave me the impression of a warm, passionate, intense knowledge of men; he wrote as one who lived with ordinary men and knew them through and through. Yet I fancy that *The Red Horizon*, popular as it was, did not have the sales of *The First Hundred Thousand*.

I was lunching with Professor John Adams one day in London. We got on to the subject of circulations, and he said that he had just been asking the biggest bookseller in London what novel sold best.

"Have a guess," said the Professor to me.

"*David Copperfield*," I said promptly.

He laughed.

"Not bad!" he said, "you've got the author right, but the book is *A Tale of Two Cities*."

He then asked me to guess what two authors sold best among the troops at the front during the war.

"Charles Garvice and Nat Gould," I said, and the Professor thought me a wonderful fellow, for I had guessed aright.

There is a whiskered Ford story which tells that Mr. Ford took a new car from his factory and invited a visitor to have a spin. They started off, and went seven miles out. Then the car stopped. Ford jumped out and lifted the bonnet.

"Good Lord!" he cried, "the engine hasn't been put in! The car must have run seven miles on its reputation!"

I think that books run many miles on reputation alone. Like a snowball the farther a circulation rolls the more it gathers to itself. But what is it that makes a book popular? The best press notices in the world will not send the circulation of a book up to a hundred thousand level. What sells a book is talk. Scores of people said to me: "Oh, *have* you read *The Young Visitors*?" I hasten to add, as a Scot, that I personally did not help to increase the circulation; I borrowed the book from an enthusiast. Talk sells a book, but we have to discover why people talk about *The Young Visitors* and not about—er—*The Booming of Bunkie*. The book that is to sell well must be able to touch a chord in the crowd heart, and *The Young Visitors* sold because it touched the infantile chord in the crowd heart; it brought back the happiest days of life, the schooldays: again, its naïve Malapropisms appealed to the crowd, because we are all glad to laugh at the social and grammatical errors we have made and conveniently forgotten about.

Bunkie did not reach the hundred thousand level because it was too clever; it was a purely intellectual essay in wit rather than humour. And the crowd distrusts wit, and that is why the witty plays of Oscar Wilde are seldom produced, while *Charley's Aunt* goes on for ever.

I am tempted to go on to a comparison of wit with humour, but I shall only remark that wit is an intellectual thing, whereas humour is emotional. Humour is elemental, but wit is cultural. Without a language you could have humour, but without language there could be no wit.

* * * * *

I have just come across a small book entitled *Hints on School Discipline*, by Ernest F. Row, B.Sc.

"Boys will only respect a master whom they fear," he says. I have been preaching this doctrine for years . . . that respect always has fear behind it . . . and it pleases me to find that an exponent of the old methods should support my argument.

When I began to read the book I was amazed.

"Good Lord!" I cried, "this chap should have published his book in the year 1820. He advocates a system that modern psychology has shown to be fatal to the child. It is army discipline applied to schools."

I found it hard to finish the book, but I read every word of it and then I said to myself: "The majority is on the side of Row. Eton, Harrow, many elementary teachers would agree with him. He is evidently an honest sort of fellow, and he must be reckoned with. I must try to see his point of view."

And I think I see it. He accepts current education with its set subjects, time-tables, order, morality, and he is trying to adapt the young teacher to what is established. Hence to maintain all these things, we must have stern discipline and swift punishment. But I wonder if Row has thought of the other side of the question; I wonder if he has asked himself whether order and time-tables and obedience and respect are really necessary. I should like to meet him and have a chat; I think I should like him, and further, I think that I could convert him to the other way . . . if he is under forty.

Ah! Horrid thought! Is it possible that Row is pulling our legs? No, he writes as an honest man. Perhaps he knows all about the modern movement; perhaps he has studied Montessori, Freud, Jung, Homer Lane, Edmond Holmes, and found that they are all pathetically wrong. Mayhap he has proved that the child *is* a sinner.

"The young teacher should never address a boy by his Christian name or nickname," he says.

Oh, surely he *is* pulling our legs!

* * * * *

At intervals during the past few years I have been puzzled when people congratulated me on my village school in Lancashire. I had quite a number of misunderstandings on the subject. Then one day I discovered that there was a village schoolmaster in Lancashire called E. F. O'Neill. I wrote him telling him that I was coming to see his school, and one July morning I alighted at one of the ugliest villages in the world, and I walked past slag-heaps and all the horrors of industrialism to a red building on the outskirts. Three or four boys were digging in the school garden. I walked into the school, and two seconds after entering I said to myself: "E. F. O'Neill, you are a great man!"

There were no desks, and I could see no teacher. Half-a-dozen children stood round a table weighing things and cutting things.

"What's this?" I asked.

"The shop," said a girl, and after a little time I grasped the idea. You have paste-board coins, and you come to the shop and buy a pound of butter (plasticene), two pounds of sugar (sand), and a bottle of Yorkshire Relish (a brown mixture unrecognisable to me). You pay your sovereign and the shop-keeper gives you the change, remarks on the likelihood of the weather's keeping up, and turns to the next customer.

I walked on and found a boy writing.

"Hullo, sonny, what are you on?"

"My novel," he said, and showed me the beginning of chapter XII.

A young man came forward, a slim youth with twinkling eyes.

"E. F. O'Neill?"

"A. S. Neill?"

We shook hands, and then he began to talk. I wanted to tell him that his school was a pure delight, but I couldn't get a word in edgeways. If anything, he was over-explanatory, but I pardoned him, for I realised that the poor man's life must be spent in explaining himself to unbelievers. I disliked his tacit classing of me with the infidel, and I indignantly took the side of the infidel and asked him questions. Then he gave me of his best.

He is a great man. I don't think he has any theoretical knowledge, and I believe that anyone could trip him up over Freud or Jung, Montessori or Froebel, Dewey or Homer Lane; but the man seems to know it all by instinct or intuition. To him creation is everything. I was half afraid that he might have the typical crank's belief in imposing his taste on the pupils, and I mentioned my doubt.

"No," he said, "we have a gramophone with fox-trots, ragtimes, Beethoven and Melba, and the children nearly always choose the best records."

Love of beauty is a real thing in this school. The playground is full of bonny corners with flowers and bushes. The school writing books are bound in artistic wallpaper by the children, and hand-made frames enclose reproductions of good pictures on the walls.

I saw no corporate teaching, and I should have asked O'Neill if he had any. If he hasn't I think he is wrong, for the other way—the learn-by-doing individual way—starves the group spirit. The class-teaching system has many faults, and O'Neill seems to have abolished spoon-feeding, but the class has one merit—it is a crowd. Each child measures himself against the others, not necessarily in competition. Perhaps it is the psychological effect of having an audience that I am trying to praise. Yes, that is it: the individual-work way is like a rehearsal of a play to empty seats; the class-way is like a performance before a crowded house. It is a projection of one's ego outward.

"This method," said O'Neill, "may be out-of-date in a month."

I think highly of him for these words alone. He has no fixed beliefs about methods of study; he himself learns by doing, and to-morrow will be cheerfully willing to scrap the method he is using to-day. If the ideal teacher is the man who is always learning, then O'Neill comes pretty near that ideal. I wish that every teacher in Britain could see his school.

The big problem for the heretical teacher is the problem of order, or rather of disorder. When a child is free from authority, he usually leaves his path untidy; he leaves his chisels on the bench or the ground; he strews the floor with papers; he throws his books all over the room. Now O'Neill's school was not untidy, and I marvelled.

"Oh, the kiddies look after that," he explained. "They have voluntary workers among themselves who do all that, and if a child does not do his job, the others naturally complain: 'Why did you take it on if you aren't going to do it properly?'"

But somehow I am not convinced; I want to know more about this business. To find so highly developed a social sense in small children runs dead against all my experience. I must write to O'Neill for further information.

* * * * *

On re-reading the pages of this book I feel like throwing it on the fire. I find myself disagreeing with the statements I made a few weeks ago. When I began to write it I was a more or less complete Freudian, and in an airy fashion I explained away my actions. Why should pale blue be my favourite colour? I asked myself this when I painted my cycle blue, and I found a ready answer in a reminiscence . . . my first sweetheart wore a blue tam-o'-shanter. This is called the "nothing but" psychology. Do I dream of a train? Quite simple! It is merely "nothing but" a sexual symbol!

Life is too complex for a "nothing but" psychology. Last night a girl told me a sexual dream she had had, but when she gave her associations we found that the deep meaning of the dream had nothing to do with sex. Freud says that about every dream is the mark of the beast, but then I think he believes in original sin.

I have been thinking a lot recently about the psychology of flogging. It is generally stated that the flogger is a sexual pervert, a Sadist, and undoubtedly there are pathological cases where men find sexual gratification in inflicting or in watching the infliction of pain. In the pathological case the gratification is conscious, but I believe that many respectable parents and teachers find an unconscious gratification. It is absurd to say to a man like Macdonald: "Your punishing is 'nothing but' Sadism." Yet I think that a little test might decide the matter. If the accused flogger is shocked or indignant at the idea I should be inclined to think that the accusation was a just one.

If I say to Simpson: "Excuse my mentioning it, old man, but I don't think you love your wife," he will laugh heartily, for he has been married for a month only, and is still very much in love. His laugh shows that his love is real; my rude remark touches no chord in his unconscious. But suppose I make a similar remark to Smith, who has been very much married for ten years! He will hit me in the eye, thereby betraying the fact that my remark touched what his unconscious knows to be true. His blow is physically directed to me, but psychically he is hitting to defend his conscious from his unconscious.

Hence if a flogger is angry when I accuse him of being a Sadist, I guess that he is a Sadist.

I tried the experiment on Macdonald. He shook his head sadly.

"Poor chap," he said feelingly, "you're daft!"

"Right!" I said, "you aren't a Sadist, anyway, Mac. You must flog because it is your method of self-assertion. As I've told you many times, you strap kids because wielding a strap is your childish way of showing your power."

Then Mac became angry, and when I hinted that my remarks must have hit the bull's-eye . . . he laughed again. He is a baffling study in psychology.

"You don't know much about it, old chap," he said genially.

"Hardly anything at all," I said with true modesty, "only I know one thing about you, and that is that the fault always lies in yourself. When you flog Tom Murray, you are really chastising the Tom Murray in yourself . . . that is, the part that your wife knows so well—the part of you that leaves the new graip out in the rain all night, that rebels against the authority of the School Board and the inspectorate. Tom is being crucified for your transgressions."

Barrie, wizard as he is, failed to understand the full significance of Shakespeare's line: "The fault, dear Brutus, lies not in our stars, but in ourselves."

* * * * *

The opposite of the Sadist is the Masochist—the person who finds sexual gratification in being beaten or bullied. When 'Arriet proudly boasts about the black eye that 'Arry gave her on Saturday night, she is being masochistic, and the woman who likes to be bullied by the strong, silent man is likewise a masochist. I do not say "nothing but" a masochist, because she is also a Sadist, for Sadism and Masochism are complementary in the same person.

It is an understood fact that many people find joy in suffering, and I can recollect feeling something akin to joy when the dentist, before the days of the local anaesthetic, used to lay hold on my molars.

Hence I look back to the day when I whacked Peter Smith for cruelty to a calf, and I acknowledge that I was wrong. I recall explaining to him that I wanted him to realise what suffering meant, but I was completely mistaken. If Peter were a Sadist in his cruelty, my cruelty to him was giving unconscious gratification to the Masochistic part of him. If his cruelty to the calf was due to his self-assertion again I did the wrong thing, for the fear evoked by my strap merely inhibited his desire to assert himself in cudgelling calves. I think now that there was nothing to be done; his cruelty showed that his whole education had been wrong. Had he been allowed to create all the way up from one week old he would have applied his interest to making rabbit-hutches instead of to beating calves.

I remember a questioner at one of my lectures. I had been trying to elaborate the release theory, and had said that a boy should be encouraged to make a noise so that he will release all his interest in noise as power.

"If a boy liked torturing cats, would you encourage him on the theory that suppression by an adult would cause the child to retain his interest in torturing cats?"

"Certainly not," I said, and the lady crowed. I do dislike questioners at any time, but when they crow . . . .! However, I tried to hide the murder in my heart by smiling.

"What would you do?" she asked sweetly.

"I don't know, madam," I said, "but I can make a rapid guess . . . I very probably would use the toe of my boot on him, thereby showing that my own interest in cruelty was still alive. But five minutes later I should try to discover what was at the back of the boy's mind."

Not long ago I studied a small boy whose chief pleasure was in pulling bees' wings off. I never mentioned bees to him, but I got him to talk about himself. He was suffering from a deep hatred of his teacher, and he had a bad inferiority complex. He feared to play games like football and hockey because of his sense of inferiority. All that was wrong with him was that he was regressing. Life was too difficult for him, and he took refuge in his infantile past; his pulling off wings was the destructiveness of the infant. But the important thing to remember is that destructiveness is simply constructiveness gone wrong. The child is born good, and all his instincts are to do good. Bad behaviour is the result of thwarted desire to do good. This is shown in the case of Tommy on page 53.

* * * * *

At one time I was absolutely certain that the Great War was caused by economic factors; British and German capital were competing, and the losing party took up the sword. I am not so certain now. It may be that the cataclysm was a natural ebullition of human nature, and as a cause the economic rivalry may have been just as insignificant as the murder of the Archduke.

During the last few decades education has been almost wholly intellectual and material; intellectual education gave us the don, and material education gave us the cotton-spinner. The emotional and the spiritual in mankind had no outlet. In the unconscious of man there is a God and a Devil, and intellectual activities afford no means of expression to either. And when any godlike or devilish libido can find no outlet it regresses to infantile primitive forms; thus, while the brain of man was concerned with mathematics and logic, the heart of man was seeking primitive things—cruelty, hate, and blood.

It may be then that the war was the direct result of the world's bad system of education. No boy will destroy property if he is free to create property, and no nation will take to killing if it is free to be creative. Intellectual education allows no freedom for the creative impulse; it not only starves the creative impulse but it drives it into rebellion. An outlet is always a door to purification. The old men who sat at home hated the Hun because their libido was being bottled up, but the young men who were using up their libido in fighting talked cheerfully of "Old Fritz." The chained dog soon becomes savage, and the chained libido reverts to savagery also.

I have often said that the outrages of the German troops in Belgium became understandable to me when I studied a Scots school where suppressive discipline turned good boys into demons. The brutality of the German army was a natural result of the brutality of their discipline. So is it in the individual soul, and in the national soul. Intellectualism and materialism were the Prussian drill-sergeants who enslaved the emotional life of the citizen and of the nation. War was a means of releasing this pent-up emotion.

The ultimate cure for war is the releasing of the beast in the heart of mankind . . . not the releasing after chaining him up, but the releasing of the beast from the beginning. Personally I do not believe that he is a wild beast until we make him one by chaining him; he is primitive and animal and amoral, but I believe that by kind treatment we can make him our ally in living a goodly life. The Devil is merely a chained God.

The problem for man and for mankind is to reconcile the God and the Devil in himself. The saint represses the devil; the sinner represses the god. The atheist cries: "There is no God!" because he has repressed the God in himself. Then, again, many people project their personal devil; the men who shouted "Hang the Kaiser!" were subjectively crying "Hang the Devil in me!"

Who and what is this devil we carry in our hearts? We cannot tame him unless we can know him. The Freudians would say that he is the primitive unconscious, the tree-dweller in us. But that explanation is not enough for me. The tiger has no devil in him, and why should our remote savage ancestors leave us a devil as legacy? Yet the tiger is a devil whenever man formulates a law against killing; the man-eater becomes bad because he is a danger to man, and because the tiger is bad it is assumed that man is good. The ox that is slaughtered for our dinners might well look upon man as its special objective devil.

I have often argued that it is Authority that makes the beast in children a wild beast. That is true, but it does not go down to first causes. Why do adults exercise authority? To keep down the devil in themselves, the beast that *their* parents and teachers made wild by authority. Truly a vicious circle! But the devil is the cause of authority in the beginning.

Since there is no devil in the tiger and the ox, the animalism of man cannot be his devil. But man made his animalism a devil when he began to have ideals. Then it was that he began to talk of crucifying the flesh; then it was that the spirit was willing but the flesh was weak. The devil in man is the negative of man's ego-ideal. The ethical self says that honesty is good, and dishonesty comes to be of the devil; it says that love is good, and hate then becomes devilish. No ego-ideal, no devil. The ox has no ego-ideal; therefore it has no devil. Man invented the devil to account for his failures.

This brings me to the question: why should man want to have an ego-ideal?

Why should he praise self-sacrifice, love, charity, honesty, unselfishness, while he contemns hate, murder, cruelty, stealing, selfishness? It might be argued that he praises those attributes that make for the good of the herd, but I cannot take this argument as final. Rather am I inclined to look for the answer in what we vaguely call the divine. I think that there is a power . . . call it God or intuition or the superconscious or what-not . . . that draws man toward higher things. This spark of the divine raises man above the beast of the field, but yesterday he was the beast of the field, and like the *nouveau riche*, he scorns his humble origins.

I am forced to conclude that wars will not cease until man realises that his ego-ideal must be capable of being the working partner of his primitive animalism. When that time comes man will know that he is neither god nor devil, but . . . mere man.

* * * * *

I am spending my days wandering round London suburbs looking for a school. Of an evening I sit and think about how I shall furnish it. There will be no desks; instead there will be tables for writing and drawing on, chairs of all descriptions—arm-chairs, deck-chairs, straight backed chairs, stools. The children will make the tables and stools, and we may make a combined effort to make and upholster an arm-chair.

Then we must have at least one typewriter, not for office use, but for the children's use. The children will use it to type their novels and poems, and I think they would be tempted to type out poems from Keats and Coleridge, binding their own anthologies in leather or coloured paper.

There will be no school readers and no school poetry books. I hope that with the aid of the typewriter each child will make his own selection of prose and poetry.

The wall decorations will be left to the children, and if they bring bad, sentimental prints from the Christmas numbers I shall say nothing when they hang them up. But as an active member of the community, I shall bring reproductions of the work of Rembrandt, Velasquez, Angelo, Augustus John Cezanne, Nevinson; I shall buy *Colour* every month.

So with music. I shall sing *Eliza Jane* with them if they want to sing *Eliza Jane*, but I shall bring to their notice *To Music* (Schumann), Blake's *Jerusalem*, and the bonny old English songs like *Golden Slumbers, Now is the Month of Maying, Polly Oliver*. Then a gramophone is a necessity, and all kinds of records will be necessary—Beethoven, Stravinsky, Rimski-Korsikoff, Harry Lauder, Fox Trots, Sousa. O'Neill told me that his Lancashire kiddies have tired of ragtime, and are now playing classical music only. Personally, I haven't reached that standard of taste yet; I still have Fox Trot moods. I also want a player-piano—an Angelus, if possible.

Now for the library. I shall leave the choice of periodicals to the community, and I expect to find them select a list of this kind:—*Scout, Boy's Own Paper, Girl's Own Paper, Popular Mechanics, My Magazine, Punch, Chips, Comic Cuts, Tit-Bits, Answers, Strand, Sketch, Sphere*. It will be interesting to watch the career of *Chips*; I will not be surprised if the community tires of *Chips* in a month.

Our book library will be stocked from the children's homes, I fancy. Each child will bring his or her favourite novel, and gladly hand it round. I shall certainly hand on my own fiction library:—Conan Doyle, Wells, Jack London, Rider Haggard, Cutcliffe Hyne, Guy Boothby, Barrie, O. Henry, Leacock, Jacobs, Leonard Merrick, Seton Merriman, Stanley Weyman, and a host of others.

No, this won't do! How can I furnish before my self-governing school decides what furniture it will have? The children may demand desks and time-tables, but I do not think it likely. Anyhow, I am counting my chickens before they are hatched.

XIV.

I finish this book in the place where I began it, in Forfarshire, but not in Tarbonny Village. Hustling Herbert Jenkins sent me the galley proofs this morning with an urgent demand that I should return them at once. I do dislike publishers. At first I took them at their own valuation: I believed what they said.

"Machines waiting," Jenkins would wire. "Send MS. at once."

And I, simple I, would sit up late correcting proofs. I know better now. I know that Jenkins always divides time by 20. His "at once" means that twenty days hence he will say to his Secretary: "That new book of Neill's . . . has it gone to the printer yet?" And his Secretary will 'phone down to the office secretary and say: "You've got to send Neill's new book to the printer." Then this lady will order the office-boy to take the MS. to the printer . . . and I bet the little devil reads *Deadwood Dick on the Boomerang Prairie* as he crawls to the printer's office with my masterpiece under his arm.

Hence, understanding Jenkins, I tossed the proofs into a corner this morning, and went out to continue the game of ring quoits that Nellie and I had to give up as darkness fell last night. Nellie is a Dundee lassie of thirteen and she is spending her holidays with her auntie here.

Nellie won, and we sat down on the bank and I began to ask her about her school-life.

"I dinna like the school, and I wish I was left," she said.

"Tell me why you dislike it, Nellie."

"If ye speak ye get the strap."

"What!" I cried, "are you *never* allowed to speak?"

"Only at playtime," she replied. "And ye never get less than six scuds."

And it was only the other day that a lady wrote me saying that when I preach against Prussianism in schools I am merely resuscitating a dead bogey for the purpose of knocking it down.

I get quite a lot of information of schools from children. I remember when I was in Lyme Regis last Easter I went out sketching one day. As I passed a village school a troupe of happy children came out. Joy lit up their faces.

"The ideal school!" I cried, and stopped to speak to them.

"Tell me, children, tell me why you have laughter in your eyes," I said, "tell me of your happy school."

The oldest boy grinned.

"Master's gone off for the day to a funeral," he said.

I walked on deep in thought.

Nellie dislikes school. What a tragedy. She is a dear sweet child with kind eyes and a bonny smile. She spoke frankly to me at first but when I told her that I was a teacher she looked at me with fear and (I smiled at this) dropped her Dundee dialect and answered me in School English. I had to throw plantain heads at her for a full five minutes before the look of fear left her eyes and her dialect returned.

"I dinna believe ye *are* a teacher," she said to-night.

"Why not?"

"Ye're no like ane," she said hesitatingly. "Ye're ower—ower daft."

"But why shouldn't a teacher be daft?" I asked.

"They shud be respectable," she said, "or the children winna respect them."

I looked alarmed.

"What!" I cried, "don't you respect me?"

She laughed gaily.

"No!" she cried, then she added seriously: "But I'd like to be at your schule."

She returns to Dundee to-morrow, to a class of fifty, where silence reigns. Poor Nellie! What worries me is that when Nellie's teacher reads this book she will most probably agree with Nellie's remark that I'm "daft". But she won't mean what Nellie meant.

A telegraph girl approached.

"Machines are waiting.—Jenkins."

Nellie looked anxious.

"That's twa telegrams ye've got the day," she said. "Is onybody deid?"

I looked at the words on the telegraph form.

"No, Nellie, unfortunately no!" I said slowly, and I went in to read my galley proofs.

THE END.

9 789361 385056

Printed by Libri Plureos GmbH in Hamburg, Germany